This is for you Harmonie and Sonny.

With thanks to John John,

who pestered me for years to write it

and Fulvia Lazzar who designed the cover.

Every man desires to live long,

but no man would be old.

Jonathon Swift

Miss Older And The Ivies
A Conflict Of Interest

Prologue

Bessie was dying.
I held her hand and watched her become gradually paler and waxier as the night wore on. Again and again she took a feeble shuddering breath and lay so still, I thought it was her last one and then once or twice she opened her eyes and didn't close them for so long, I was sure she'd gone.
I kept watching her, waiting for I didn't know what sign.
I could hardly keep checking her pulse or put my face up against hers to feel for her breath or close her eyes for her, could I? I mean, what if she wasn't dead yet? It would have been rude. I did nothing. I'd 'know' when the moment came, I thought.
After a while I developed doubts and became obsessed with the idea that she might die *without* me 'knowing', that rigor mortis would set in and I wouldn't be able to get my hand free.
Eventually she stirred and I took her hand to lay it palm down by her side placing mine on top and I stroked her from time to time to let her know that I was there. It was hard to feel comfortable with a dying body, yet it was still Bessie, the lovely person I'd come to know and love. Then she moved her hand and curled one of her fingers round mine,
"You're a good girl ducks" she whispered.
I can't deny that I was afraid. I was shit scared to tell the truth. To witness a life coming to an end is an earth-shattering event after all, but I wasn't panicking. In fact I was rather pleased with how well I was coping, never having witnessed a

death before or having had any training in caring for the dying. Looking back though, it's possible the smell of lavender water I'd dabbed on her temples when she'd been restless was wafting over and keeping me calm as well as her.

As I sat there, I started wondering whether training in the subject of caring for the dying was even possible. Nobody could know how a dead person would prefer to have been treated while they were dying, could they? I asked myself whether I'd like somebody to hold *my* hand on *my* deathbed and I didn't know the answer to be honest. It would depend who was going to hold it, wouldn't it? Another thought to cross my mind was how daft it would be to have to do any of those annoying 'role play' sessions as part of any training process. They were used for everything else, so I couldn't discount the possibility.

One thing was clear to me: Bessie wasn't scared in the slightest. She knew what was happening, she embraced it and without any fuss or bother she slowly but surely faded away.

The strangest things crossed my mind during the stillness of that night. I thought of Bessie's life, my life, life itself, death itself and I thought about what the chances had been of it actually being *me* to sit with her at that time, in that place and in those particular circumstances...

Chapter 1

The minute we got stuck into running our first business, which we bought as a going concern in October 1983, my other half and I decided we most definitely, absolutely, were not, under any circumstances whatsoever, going to keep the name it had been trading under, which was 'Ivy's Rest Home'. In the first place it didn't belong to Ivy, whoever she was, and in the second place, we thought it was naff to say the least. It had the same ring as 'Joe's Caff', if you know what I mean, and although there was nothing wrong with the name Ivy, or Joe for that matter, we needed something with a more professional edge, which would better reflect the kind of establishment we intended to run. Quite frankly, a first name just wasn't going to do it for us so, after much deliberation, we renamed it 'The Ivies' and planted some different varieties of ivy into a large container, which we placed under a smart new sign. Sheer inspiration, don't you think?

Now, you'd be forgiven for thinking I must have invented the name Miss Older for the purpose of this story, but you'd be quite wrong, because she was a real person, it was her real name and she lived in the bungalow next door, though for some extraordinary reason we didn't make the word association at the time.

I was getting one of the residents, Louise to be precise, into the car about six months after moving in when I first actually spoke to her. She was hanging out her washing at the time. We'd seen each other occasionally, but had only said the odd 'hello', nothing more.

"Good morning!" she called out, peering over the fence, "Going somewhere nice?"

She was a tall good-looking lady, possibly in her eighties, with a kind face and a thick mop of white hair.

"Just the doctor's." I replied.

She looked at me with the telltale expression of a person who hadn't heard a word and was pretending she had.

4

"Nice day for it." she commented, to suit anything I might have said.

This brought a smile to my face as I closed Louise's door and walked round to the driver's side.

"Before you came," she continued. "I never saw any old people coming out." She paused while I opened the door then added with a chortle,

"Only going in!"

"Oh dear!" I shouted, throwing my bag on to the back seat.

"The house looks nice" she continued. "Good luck. I'm sure you'll be very successful."

"Thank you." I said, still smiling and getting into the car. While I fiddled with the seat belts, Louise sat watching Miss Older struggle back to her house along the uneven path with her empty washing basket.

"Poor darling." she said, tutting and shaking her head. "Look at her, poor old soul, she can hardly walk."

Louise, already well into her nineties, was extremely frail herself, having just a minute ago negotiated the front door step with great difficulty, hanging on to me for dear life, before manoeuvring her stiff legs and body into the car.

Chapter 2

As far as I could tell, Miss Older hardly ever left the house. I only saw her occasionally and nobody seemed to visit her either. She didn't appear to have a home help or regular deliveries except the milkman and the postman. She had a gardener once a week, but apart from that, she always seemed to be on her own.

It was the gardener who came over to the rest home one Friday morning, Good Friday to be precise, about eighteen months after we moved in. I remember the occasion really well, because Mrs W, in room three at the front of the house, had been invited to stay with her daughter for the whole Easter week, which was unheard of for an elderly person in care. In fact it was the first and last time we can recall it ever happening during more than twenty years in the rest home business. On my way to the front door, I passed her room and noticed her standing at the window all packed and ready to go.

"I'm sorry to trouble you." he said (the gardener that is) taking his cap off and rolling it up in the palms of his hands. "Only I don't know what to do about the old girl next door. She fell over and hurt her arm yesterday see. Lucky I was there. I usually only come on a Wednesday, but I came yesterday as well because I'll be away next week. Well I managed to get her up all right and got her to hospital in the old banger, but I couldn't stay with her, I've got me wife to worry about. Anyway I've just this minute popped in to see how she got on and she's only gone and broke the darn thing and you'll never guess what? They only sent her home in a taxi. I mean, it's Easter, she's eighty-six, she's got her arm in plaster and she's got nobody. How's she supposed to manage? I can't look after her."

He was quite elderly himself and I could see he was in a bit of a panic.

"Come on in," I said "Let's see what we can do"

"Thanks all the same," he replied unrolling his cap and putting it back on "got to get going, got the wife in the car. She's chair bound, see. I know you'll do the right thing. Her name's Miss Older. Thanks again. Bye then."
Shit, I was looking forward to a nice quiet Easter.

Chapter 3

I left my husband and my daughter making elevenses, or to be more precise half *tenses*, and went next door. When I got there, the front door was wide open and I could see Miss Older sitting in her living room right ahead of me at the end of the hall.

The air was stale and the place was dark and dingy, but it looked tidy and cared for. I called out to her as I walked in, introducing myself along the way.

"Hello Miss Older, it's Sonia from the rest home next door."

"Sandra?"

"No, SONIA"

"Sorry dear, did you say Silvia?" she held out her good hand, the left one and I took hold of it laughing.

"No, S-<u>O</u>-N-<u>EE</u>-A"

"S-O-N-EE-A" she repeated, squeezing my hand. "Oh, Soneea, I am glad to see you. I knew you'd come. I told Stan to get you. I told him you'd know what to do. Oh I am glad you're here. I had such a fall. Look what I've done."

It was as if she'd known me all her life.

She looked awful, she didn't have her bottom teeth in, her hair was all over the place and she was pale and drawn.

"Don't worry." I said "We'll sort you out"

I had no idea how, because we didn't have a vacancy and were already rushed off our feet, but for some reason I felt responsible for her.

"We'll put more water in it next time." I added flippantly and she beamed a toothless smile at me, squeezing my hand tighter.

"Sit yourself down dear." she said "Here, would you like a cigarette?" She was delighted when I accepted and we sat smoking together while she told me what happened. When she got to the bit about being sent home in a taxi, I told her I thought it very odd for casualty to discharge an elderly person in her circumstances.

"They wanted to keep me in," she explained, looking straight into my eyes " but I told them I had you right next door and that's why they let me out."
Well blow me down!

Chapter 4

It occurred to me that the sensible thing to do was to invite Miss Older to lunch.

She'd be in a safe environment while I'd be able to talk it over with my family and see if we could come up with a plan.

She loved the idea of coming over for lunch, but would need help to go to the loo and get washed and changed. I said I'd have to pop home and let the others know, I'd make her a nice cup of tea first and be right back.

"Can you hang on?" I asked.

"Ooh yes dear." she replied excitedly.

Walking back up the drive I met Mrs W's daughter Veronica parking her car. She was in a right old flap because she'd got stuck in traffic and was a bit late. You'd have thought it was a real disaster, but she always did take things rather seriously. When I told her that the lady next door had fallen the previous morning breaking her arm and hadn't been able to get herself up, so had been forced to stay on the floor until her gardener arrived at two in the afternoon, she stopped being in a right old flap.

Mrs W. was at the window waving excitedly and came towards us as soon as we stepped into the house. I was disappointed to notice she was still wearing her green pinny. She always wore it and walked about with her hands in the pockets, fiddling with sweets and sweet papers. I'd suggested she take it off to look nice and smart for Veronica. Anyway, as she walked towards us, she almost ignored her altogether even though she hadn't seen her for some time and asked how the 'Old girl' next door was getting on, having evidently heard some of the conversation with the gardener earlier.

Then, without conferring, they both came up with the same possible solution: couldn't she have Mrs W's place in room three?

10

It was as if the hand of fate had decided on the exact chain of events, which would inexorably lead to Miss Older becoming a big part of our lives.

I thought about it for a moment and was warmed by their generosity and the fact that they both instinctively wanted to help.

"Well, it *is* a good idea." I said "Are you sure you don't mind?"

"Hello!" beamed my old man, emerging from the resident's lounge, "Anyone else for coffee?"

"Ooh yes please." we all said in unison.

Chapter 5

Leaving Mrs W and Veronica to drink their coffee, we went through to the kitchen, which was for staff only.

During this period we were calling my old man Wanty Wanty, a nickname I'd recently discovered his aunts and uncles gave him when he was little, which I thought was hysterical and we were calling my daughter Tess, because this was her stage name in the band she was singing in at the time.

Anyway, the three of us sat round the kitchen table and discussed Miss Older's situation and drew up the following list of things to do:

1. Collect her before lunch for a glass of sherry.
2. Establish whether she wants to come and stay.
3. If she does, admit her as temporary resident.
4. Fill in admission form and other paperwork.
5. Make a list of things she wants to bring over.
6. Locate her medical card.
7. Arrange a home visit from her G.P. meanwhile start her on a course of calcium tablets.
8. Change Mrs W's bed removing personal belongings.
9. Spend time with Mrs Swain, the other lady in room three, explain the situation and involve her where possible.
10. Introduce Miss Older and Mrs Swain at 3.30pm. Serve afternoon tea in their room and give them the opportunity to get to know each other.

We were already overworked and underpaid and realised this would put a strain on our resources, but we could hardly refuse to help a neighbour, so we took out a new folder, got the paper work ready and stuck the list on the board to tick off the items as they got done.

Then Veronica knocked on the kitchen door to tell us she was ready to leave. Mrs W was waiting at the front door with her coat and scarf on, clutching her handbag.

Tess said goodbye to them both and went off to collect the cups, Wanty Wanty took the suitcase and I helped Mrs W into the car. As she settled into the seat, her coat gaped open and yep, there it was still, that flipping green pinny!

Chapter 6

The rest home was registered for eight permanent residents. 'Category: Elderly'.

The house was a Victorian semi, converted into two double and four single letting rooms spread out equally over the two floors.

The residents' lounge/diner was on the ground floor and a modern extension at the back of the house comprised the kitchen, utility room and the owner's two bedroom, self-contained flat.

The residents' bathroom with toilet was upstairs, as was the separate loo.

One of the requirements for registration was a chair lift, which we had installed as soon as we took over, so that not having ground floor facilities didn't present any problems for less mobile residents.

By the time Miss Older came into our lives, we'd completely redecorated inside and outside, re-carpeted the whole house, re-furnished every room and installed vanity units in the letting rooms. We'd taken the disgusting old kitchen out, replaced every single thing in it and we'd bought new bedding and linen. In the double rooms we'd arranged the furniture in such a way as to create two separate areas with a curtain, which could be drawn for privacy.

It was a light, airy house with high ceilings and interesting features and I was really proud of our achievements, I was also confident that Miss Older would like the warm atmosphere and find a friendly welcome as well as a safe environment.

For the time being at least.

Chapter 7

It was obvious from the start that I'd be the one to be allocated the job of collecting Miss Older, since I was the only one of us she'd met. It proved to be a memorable challenge and took bloody ages.

In the loo, with only the one hand available, she was having trouble holding her skirt up at the same time as pulling her bloomers down and she called me in to help. I held her skirt up while we both struggled with her enormous baggy long johns, which had somehow got twisted and stuck into the zip of her skirt, then, following her instructions, I went into the bedroom to look for her bottom teeth, which had apparently shot out of her mouth the day before when she'd lost her balance while making the bed.

I peered under the bed on all fours, but it was too dark and I had to get up and go and draw the curtains. Back in the crawling position, I spotted them at the far end of the room under the chest of drawers. I got up again and tried to reach them, but in order to do so I needed to lie flat on my stomach, which I really didn't fancy, so I had to get up yet again and go and find a broom and try to sweep them out. It wasn't easy because the chest of drawers was a huge piece of antique furniture placed across a corner of the room with a standard lamp behind it, and the damned denture was wedged in between the base of the lamp and one of the back legs. Anyway I managed it in the end and found that it was covered in dust, so I had to rinse it in the kitchen when I took the broom back.

I was beginning to feel just a little bit cheesed off by now, especially when I remembered the teacup in the living room I couldn't really leave unwashed.

Meanwhile, Miss Older had made her way into the bathroom and was sitting on a stool at the sink.

"If you could help me to get these clothes off," she called out "I think I might wear a dress."

I handed her the teeth and tried to hide my bad mood by cracking the usual old joke about them trying to bite me and carefully undid the sling.

"If you could undo my bra dear, I'll have a good wash."

Bra? She wasn't wearing a *bra,* she was wearing bloody body armour, an amazing indestructible monstrosity she must have had for over half a century with metal inserts in every single seam and a good fifteen hooks and eyes running down the back panel, which were practically impossible to prise open.

"How on earth do you get this blooming thing on?" I asked, not in the least bit interested in her answer.

"What you do is, you wrap it round your waist, back to front, you do the hooks up, then you twist it back round and you put your arms through the straps. It's easy once you get the knack, as long as you don't get it upside down and you've got two hands."

As much as I liked her and thought it was actually quite funny, I didn't need this. I'd seen it all before. The ridiculous, completely useless, unnecessary, debilitating array of old people's undergarments. What I did need was to hurry up. It was fast approaching lunchtime and I was getting irritable.

"Well you haven't got two hands." I said, a little more harshly than I intended. "So what about a vest?"

"If you think so dear. There's one in the top drawer in the bedroom and it might be quicker if you choose a dress while you're there."

She'd got the message and was going to be as accommodating as possible so as not to risk upsetting me. I was so ashamed of myself I could have burst into tears.

Once she was dressed and ready with her hair brushed, we collected her coat and handbag in silence and, as we walked the short distance to the rest home, I tried to make amends by stopping to admire the daffodils in her front garden, but the more I said, the more crass and insincere I sounded and, if I could only turn the clock back, I'd delete this episode altogether.

16

In the event, I stepped over the threshold first and turned to face her holding out my hands to help her. "There we are." I said, in what came out as a rather fake jolly sort of voice, persisting as I was with my attempt to smooth things over, but she avoided eye contact and I knew for sure I'd really hurt her feelings.

I'd always promised myself not to turn into a typical hardnosed matron, bullying everyone into submission, yet in that short space of time I'd been very unkind and completely insensitive towards a vulnerable defenceless old lady, a classic bully I'd say. Well done, Sonia!

The very reason we'd chosen the care home business was because we thought we could do it so much better than those we'd seen and we believed we could really make a difference.

For example, we'd picked up from experience that people needing care, for whatever reason, benefit above all from continuity, because familiar faces, routines and methods make people feel safe and happy, which goes a long way towards their general well being. In light of this, we didn't use temporary or agency staff and we made it our business to get to know as much as possible about each individual, avoiding the use of endless lists and care plans. We got to know all about their likes and dislikes, where they came from, who their relatives were and what their interests were. We got to know who didn't like coffee or tomato soup or Brussels sprouts. We didn't need nametags in their clothing, because we got to recognise what belonged to whom, we even got to know what medication each resident was on and had a good knowledge of their medical history, just like a proper family.

Another thing was the way we decorated and furnished the house. We didn't buy anything from wholesalers or trade magazines and I personally made all the curtains and cushions, choosing fabrics I would have liked in my own home. We didn't put ugly notices all over the place, you know, like 'STAFF ONLY' 'OFFICE' 'TOILET' 'NOW WASH YOUR HANDS' etc. We had framed pictures on the walls, tasteful ornaments, potted plants and residents were encouraged to bring items of their own furniture, so as to create an atmosphere of genuine domesticity.

To avoid looking like bog standard carers in ghastly nylon overalls and black lace up shoes, I made white cotton aprons for us girls to wear. They had frills on the shoulder straps, which crossed over at the back into fat bows. They were always beautifully starched and we wore gathered black skirts and t-shirts underneath with plimsolls or ballet pumps on our feet. Wanty-Wanty looked smart, but relaxed in black trousers and a white short sleeve shirt.

We kept everything immaculately clean, using ordinary domestic products, never commercial disinfectants or air fresheners and visitors always said the house didn't smell or look like the average care home.

Well, getting the appearances and the principles of care right turned out to be the easy bit. Putting it all into practice was a different kettle of fish and this was brought painfully home to me now, when I helped Miss Older out of her coat and handed over her handbag, because she avoided looking at me again and remained silent.

Seeing the expression on her face and how miserable I'd made her feel, I understood for the first time how easy it was to lose your humanity when similar scenes were repeated over and over again. Was this the beginning of the slippery slope towards becoming another hardnosed matron? I wasn't prepared to let that happen, so I took hold of her hands and said with genuine regret,

"I'm ever so sorry, Miss Older, I didn't mean to upset you earlier." She still wouldn't look at me, but I kept hold of her hands just the same.

"Honestly I didn't, I'm just a nasty piece of work." I added.

"Of course you're not dear. I shouldn't have expected you to drop everything."

And she looked at me and gave me a proper toothy smile, squeezing my hands, so I knew she'd forgiven me and we were firm friends.

18

Chapter 8

Elderly people with hearing difficulties have a tendency to tune into and out of various wavelengths: one minute they can hear everything, the next minute nothing at all. Many a frustrated relative would accuse residents of only hearing what they wanted to hear. This was known as 'selective hearing', but in my experience it wasn't as simple as that, because in familiar surroundings and happy situations the elderly hard of hearing were more confident and relaxed and were more likely to hear quite well, whereas unfamiliar places or difficult circumstances could bring on sudden bouts of profound deafness.

To prove my point Miss Older had tuned in to my wavelength. She was hearing me better than when I'd introduced myself earlier and I wasn't having to repeat myself, but now that she was on new territory and Wanty-Wanty was bouncing down the stairs saying something with an outstretched hand, she looked to me for a translation. When I told her what he'd said, which was: "Hello there, you must be the daft old codger from next door," she burst out laughing and I knew at once that she liked him and felt at home with us both.

This sort of disrespectful language was seriously in breach of 'National Guidelines', as was using pet names, but my old man was just being himself and that's what the old codgers loved about him. He took hold of her arm leading her along.

"Nice glass of sherry my dear?"

She had absolutely no trouble hearing that!

Chapter 9

The only resident in the lounge at the time of Miss Older's arrival was Louise, who had senile dementia. This was a lucky coincidence, firstly because they'd seen each other before, so they both had a point of reference and secondly because meeting more than one person at a time can be daunting for elderly people. I can't deny feeling a sense of relief as well, knowing as I did that introducing *deaf* or *confused* elderly people to each other was always going to be a time-consuming and very trying business and I didn't want my patience to be tried again. Not only that, having left Wanty Wanty and Tess doing my tasks as well as their own, I was sure they'd be all behind and any minute now there'd be a sudden rush. I was relieved however, to see that everything was under control, the sherry, the glasses and nibbles all set out on a tray, the table laid with a vase of daffodils in the centre and a yummy smell of roast dinner wafting through from the kitchen.

While Wanty Wanty helped to get Miss Older settled into an armchair opposite Louise, rearranging the cushion behind her, I walked through and opened the kitchen door just to make sure Tess was managing on her own and suddenly Miss Older unexpectedly bellowed out to Louise and made us all stop to listen.

"HOW-DO-YOU-DO?" she said, enunciating each word with unnecessary clarity.

"I USED TO BE A FLORIST." Louise shouted back.

"FLORENCE, YOU SAY. THAT'S A NICE NAME."

" I love flowers, you know." Louise stopped shouting.

"I SEE, DEAR"

"I used to get them fresh from Covent Garden."

"FROM THE GARDEN?"

"The market Covent Garden. Do you know it?"

"MOW IT?" OH NO, NOT ANY MORE, DEAR, I'VE GOT A GARDENER WHO DOES IT ALL."

Tess and I were desperately trying not to laugh when Wanty Wanty came to the rescue with his usual effortless humour:

"Miss Older," he said, laughing loudly. "Before you so rudely interrupted, I was going to introduce you to Louise."

"OH, NOT FLORENCE?" she replied, still at the top of her voice.

"No, not Florence. When you said HOW do you do, Louise thought you said WHAT do you do, so she said she used to be a florist, she didn't say her name was Florence."

He didn't need to go on, she saw the funny side instantly. It went straight over Louise's head, but she laughed just the same to be polite. We couldn't have hoped for a better start and they both sat having their sherry and nibbles together in comfortable silence.

Chapter 10

Ninety nine per cent of the old people in our care at any given time had two things in common: they didn't want to be in care and…they didn't like old people! As a result, getting residents to leave their rooms and be together was a challenge we faced on a daily basis. Take Bessie for example in number five, who was a hundred and one years old when we took over, mobile with a walking frame, fairly independent and self-caring, her response to coming downstairs was always the same:

"What for? I've got everything I need in me own room, ta very much. The day I go down them stairs, I'll be in me wooden box."

Even with the newly installed chair lift and a pianist employed to play on Friday afternoons, she couldn't be persuaded.

"I don't mind riding up and down on your stair thingummy, if you insist, but if you think I'm gonna sit with all them smelly old fogies, singing 'My Old Man Said Follow The Van' all afternoon, you've got another think coming."

You had to respect a centenarian with her wit, so she never did come down and Miss Older never got to meet her.

Then there was Edith in number six with advanced senile dementia, all sweetness and smiles one minute and loud outbursts of abusive ramblings the next. Her response to going downstairs went something like this:

"I don't think so, darling, not today, you're so kind to ask" and she'd look at me and reach out to hold my hand or stroke my arm. "Aren't you lovely, such smooth skin, bless you."

Alternatively, it went something like this:

"Look…..LOOK!….it's him again. He's on that bloody roof….Paderewski the old bugger….get down, get down I tell you …. HELP!…HELP! POLICE!"

So in reality there was a maximum of only six possible residents in the lounge and it only needed one to have a visitor or to be out and another to be feeling unwell for the place to look quite depleted.

My previous perception of rest homes with smiling old dears doing jigsaw puzzles, elderly gentlemen reading newspapers and friendly groups laughing and joking round dining tables was slightly inaccurate, formulated by fictitious photos in care home brochures, unrealistic television programmes and the expectation of over zealous registration authorities. In the real world, only the larger homes could hope to appear sociable and busy and we learned really quickly that this was never an indication of good quality care, in fact we strongly believed that smaller units worked better and we were committed to the principle of individual attention in a family environment.

Chapter 11

Getting back to sherry time on that famous Good Friday, the other residents missing in the lounge, apart from the ones already mentioned, (that is Mrs W, away for the week with her daughter; Bessie, only prepared to come down in her wooden box and Edith with the mood swings) were the Captain, who was out for the day with his family; Mrs Morris, who was unable to feed herself following a stroke; Mrs Swain, who was unwilling to put up with 'the slurping, munching, and gulping noises of other people eating' and finally Florence, who was never ready to appear until the food was actually on the table.

Anyway, about half an hour before serving any meal, it was necessary to remind residents, especially those who needed help, to go to the loo. Failure to do so always resulted in some bright spark wanting to go just as we rang the dinner bell, or, worse still, falling asleep after eating and having an embarrassing accident in the armchair.

Having established that same morning that Miss Older was very unlikely to have a weak bladder, Wanty Wanty went to get the upstairs lot sorted and I started with Louise.

"Would you like to come upstairs to powder your nose before lunch?" I asked tactfully.

"No it's alright, thank you, I've just this minute come back down" she replied graciously.

Damn! My ploy hadn't worked. There was no way she could have left the room, she simply didn't know where to go, how to work the chair lift or anything. Strangely, even though she was very senile and in a world of her own, when she was with other people, her social graces were intact. She imagined she was in a hotel or a restaurant and behaved impeccably. She sat elegantly with her legs crossed, her head up and her back straight. She was always ladylike and said please and thank you, smiling benignly, but she was in total denial about the reality of her situation and anyone who saw her or spoke to her would never have guessed she needed help with absolutely everything, including going to the loo. In fact she was especially in denial about going to the loo, which is why we had to use various ploys in spite of the fact that we had an unwritten policy not to patronize our residents. It wasn't unusual for our ploys to fail, but her short-term memory was so poor, we could literally walk away and go straight back with another ploy, which is what I had to do on this occasion.

"Somebody's left a handbag upstairs, I'm sure it looks like yours, Louise, would you like to come and see?" I asked, shunting her handbag out of sight with my foot.

That did the trick, by the time I got her to the chair lift, Tess was collecting the empty sherry glasses and, spotting the bag under the chair, brought it over knowing how precious it was to Louise, who let me take her to the loo, as if that were the original plan.

When it came to Miss Older's turn, her response was seriously funny for an eighty six year old:

"I thought you'd never ask!"

It made Tess and me fall about and Miss Older was so pleased with this unexpected reaction that she couldn't stop laughing herself, so much so that when we got to the chair lift, she couldn't concentrate on my instructions about how to use it correctly. We were making a lot of noise in the process, but we got there eventually and when we reached the top Wanty Wanty was waiting to tick us off,

"Can you keep the noise down please, you're not meant to have fun here you know."

"It's all her fault," said Miss Older.

There was a nice atmosphere and you could tell she wasn't merely relieved to be in safe hands, but genuinely happy and having fun.

"All I want is to go to the loo," she added innocently.

While she was in there, I knocked for Florence, next door in number four, to see if she was alright.

"Ooh jibber, jibber, just a minute." came the reply. "I'm not quite ready yet. Oh Lordy, don't mind me, I won't be long. Jibber, jibber."

I knew this meant she'd be a while yet, so I went back to assist Miss Older. Edith's voice, meanwhile was ringing down the corridor,

"He's on that roof again. The dirty bugger, he's got HER up there as well. Thou shalt not fornicate. Do you hear me? Thou shalt not FORNICATE."

Feeling a bit uncomfortable about this, I tried to cover up and said cheerfully:

"Oh dear, she's off again."

I needn't have bothered because Miss Older hadn't heard Edith or me. She was far too busy demonstrating how well she'd taken in my instructions about using the chair lift safely.

"Well done!" I said "Not bad for someone with a broken arm. I can see you're going to fit in nicely."

"Oh I do hope so Soneea, I'm so glad to be here. I knew I could turn to you."

You had to admire her guts. She must have had it all worked out for ages.

Chapter 12

On our way back to the lounge, I became aware that she was walking rather oddly, lifting her feet off the ground like a robot instead of peeling them off in the normal way. I knew she wasn't all that steady on her feet from seeing her in her garden, but I started to wonder whether she'd injured more than her arm when she fell. I made a mental note as I got her settled back in her chair and then I heard the chairlift being called back upstairs, which meant that Wanty Wanty was bringing Florence down, so I knew I needed to get Mrs Swain to the loo.

Everybody loved Mrs Swain: the residents, the inspectors, the chiropodist, the hairdresser, the pianist, the district nurse, the hearing aid man, in fact every single person she had contact with including or rather, especially, all of us.

She was blind and chair bound, she had a small fragile body, a huge personality and she used to sit in her armchair with the door wedged open so she could be entertained by the comings and goings of every day life. Room three, which she shared with Mrs W, had the staircase practically opposite and the front door just along a bit to the right and, as far as she was concerned, she had the best seat in the house, especially with Mrs W keeping a permanent watch at the window for any interesting happenings in the street.

"I'm her ears" she used to say about Mrs W. "and she's my eyes." Needless to say, keeping doors wedged open was in breach of fire regulations.

"I tell you what," she suggested "get the fire officer in here, blindfold him, sit him in this chair with his feet tied together and let's see how long he lasts."

It was a very attractive idea, but it was never going to demonstrate how completely unlikely it was, even for sighted and mobile elderly people, to be strong enough to open the obligatory, self closing, one hour fire doors, as well as to have the necessary speed to get through the gap before being walloped in the back and sent flying unceremoniously halfway down the corridor when they swung back.

"Surely we can find a volunteer for a practical demonstration." she said, "I'm entitled to some entertainment after all"

We laughed a lot and just kept wedging the door open.

Mrs Swain liked people to knock on the open door before entering or saying anything so that she could guess who it was. She had the amazing ability of recognizing people by the amount of noise they made when they walked, or by their scent. She so rarely got it wrong we all thought she had psychic powers. Anyway, with just about enough time to get her to the loo before lunch, I knocked on the open door.

"Ah, that must be you, Sonia." she said, before I'd even stepped into the room. She would have known that somebody was due to take her upstairs, but she couldn't have known it was definitely going to be me.

"And what makes you so sure it's me, might I ask" I enquired jovially, as I removed her meal trolley from under her feet.

"Powers of deduction. I'm not as daft as I look."

"You could never look daft, only beautiful." I told her, helping her into the standing position.

"Flattery will get you anything." she joked back.

She was too frail to manage a walking frame, so we used to hold both her hands and walk backwards leading her very gently and slowly along.

"All I want is the truth." I replied "How did you know it was me?"

We were making our way to the chair lift now, a well-rehearsed routine we did mostly on automatic pilot.

"No magical powers I'm afraid, I knew it was you, because I heard Wanty Wanty with Miss Jibber just a minute ago." There was absolutely no malice in the nickname, but we didn't encourage it in case we got used to it and started using it ourselves, not least because the use of nicknames was strictly forbidden by the registration authority. When we told her about this, she got a fit of the giggles,

"Just as well she only says 'jibber' and not the 'f' word!"

Meanwhile in the resident's lounge, while Louise was busy emptying the contents of her handbag onto the meal trolley, lining up the items after examining each one closely and wiping it with yesterday's napkin, Wanty Wanty was introducing Miss Older to Florence.

"This is the lady from next door, Florence. She's come to stay for a while because she's broken her...."
Florence interrupted before he could finish:

"You've come to the right place... you'll be well looked after here... they can't do enough for you and they know what they're doing... I should know with my bad leg I can't get about like I used to... can't even bend it see, ooh, it's real punishment... ooh jibber jibber... don't mind me I've always been a chatterbox... don't you worry ... nothing's too much trouble for any of them...they're good honest folk they are, that's for sure, and they've got a good sense of humour... always smiling, not like the other lot before... good riddance to bad rubbish, that's what I say...."
Wanty Wanty had to interrupt her otherwise she would have gone on for ages, in any case, she was going at such a speed, Miss Older's eyes had glazed over and she was fast gaining the expression of a person experiencing one of those sudden bouts of profound deafness.

"Miss Older, this is Florence. She's in number four at the top of the stairs opposite the chair lift."
I was walking into the room just as he was saying this and Miss Older looked over in my direction before saying with a knowing smile,

"Florence, you say. That *is* a nice name."

"Don't start all that again!" I pleaded.

"As long as you don't tell me she's another florist," she retorted.

"Help!" Cried Wanty Wanty "I'm surrounded by crazy women!"

"Oh Lordy, it even hurts to laugh, don't mind me, I've always liked good humour, ask anybody, ooh it does make you mad, jibber jibber…."

Chapter 13

Mealtimes were a complicated affair. Some residents needed a lot of help and were embarrassed to eat with the others, so they had their meals served on a tray in their room. Mrs Swain was one such person. She was the one who said she couldn't stand the noises other people made when they ate, but in reality, she dropped more food in her lap than she put in her mouth and was really self-conscious about it.

Mrs Morris was another such person. Left partially paralysed after her stroke, it was well over eighteen months before she regained complete mobility and when she had to be spoon-fed, she didn't want an audience.

Other residents couldn't sit at the dining table for one reason or another, so they would come down for meals, but would stay in the armchair with a meal trolley in front and they too would have their meal served on a tray. Florence, for example, couldn't keep her right knee bent for any length of time and was unable to accommodate this outstretched leg under the table without crashing into somebody else's.

Some residents were unpredictable, like Louise, who didn't like moving from her chair at the best of times. She might say something like:

"I didn't order food, thank you. I'm expecting some friends for drinks."

So instead of escorting her to the table on such an occasion, we'd bring her meal on a tray and in the few minutes it took to do this, she'd forget what she'd just said and tuck in happily.

Getting this organised in the kitchen was a question of military precision: trays seemingly all over the place were actually following a very specific system.

There was a tray with drinks, cutlery and medication for setting the dining room table. This was delivered first and on its return journey, it was used to collect the empty sherry glasses. Then the trays for those eating downstairs, but not at the dining room table, were laid out with napkins, drinks and medication in numerical order. Also in numerical order were the plates, not on trays for those eating at the table.

Finally the trays for those eating in their rooms were laid out the same as those not at the table and one last tray was laid with the saucers in a pile and the cups lined up in numerical order with the various mixtures of coffee or tea, strong or weak, milk or not, sugar or sweetener all ready to go after the meal. Easy Peasy!

We didn't need to discuss where to put Miss Older for lunch, because we all automatically knew she'd feel better with a meal trolley, being that she might find it awkward to eat with just a fork in her left hand, so her tray was set accordingly.

Wanty Wanty always got the job of sitting with residents who needed to be fed, partly because he was the best at it and partly because he could catch the horse racing on the telly, so while he was upstairs feeding Mrs Morris and before lunch was served to everybody else, I was able to sit with Miss Older for a few minutes to take down her details, find out if she had to take any tablets or if she had any particular food preferences, allergies etc and I also thought I'd take the opportunity to repay her the cigarette I'd taken earlier. When I offered her one, she told me that she only ever smoked two cigarettes a day: one around half past ten in the morning and the other after supper in the evening.

"I'll have one with you then dear," she promised apologetically.

I thought this was so civilised and quaint I tried to do it myself for a while, but I wasn't successful. I was able to give up altogether for varying lengths of time otherwise, when I smoked, I smoked full time. Of course, smoking in the dining room of a rest home seems unthinkable today, but it was the only place, apart from the lobby, where it was allowed at the time and I'm ashamed to say that I sat there smoking away as we chatted.

She told me she wasn't on any medication, although she was advised at the hospital to take paracetamol for any discomfort in her arm and she told me that she liked absolutely anything in the food department. She was very happy to be offered a bed for the week and we made a list of all the stuff she wanted me to collect from the bungalow. When I asked her where she kept her medical card, she picked up her oversized handbag from the floor, produced a large wad of letters, pension books and documents in alphabetical order, held together with an elastic band, and located it almost immediately.

I was impressed with her organizational skills and glad she didn't have a long list of complaints or medication. That she liked all types of food and had no allergies was also good news, because it meant we hadn't bitten off more than we could chew. Obviously, we were going to have to cut up her food and assist her in all her daily tasks, but it was clear to me she wasn't going to be the demanding type and wasn't going to be ringing the emergency bell all day and night. Not that we minded answering the call bell for genuine reasons, but new residents always needed extra attention until they settled in, so it was very trying if in addition they turned out to be what was known in the trade as a 'bell ringer'. Miss Older definitely wasn't going to be one of those.

Chapter 14

Planning and preparing meals for any number of elderly people was always going to be a challenge and, even for our small number of eight, a certain expertise was required.

In the first place, it was our duty to provide a healthy balanced diet with plenty of fresh fruit and vegetables as well as to make it appetizing and varied. In the second place, there were certain basic rules made by the elderly themselves, which we picked up fairly quickly: no lettuce, rocket, radishes, beetroot, aubergines, courgettes, peppers, herbs or spices. No spaghetti or pasta of any description. No curry, savoury rice or sweet and sour sauces. No chops, joints, steaks, beef burgers or tuna fish and never, ever clear soups or crusty bread rolls!

I'll never forget Bessie's reaction to spaghetti bolognaise in the really early days, for instance. Taking her lunch up one day, Tess found that she was over the other side of the room, drawing her curtains with one hand while holding on to her walking frame with the other.

"Do you want any help with that Bessie?" she asked while placing her tray on the meal trolley.

"No, I'm alright. It's too bloomin' sunny, that's all. I can't see me telly. Leave it there, ducks, ta very much."

"You've got spaghetti bolognaise and fresh fruit salad today." explained Tess brightly.

"Every time anybody comes through that door they bring me more flippin' food." replied Bessie tutting and laughing simultaneously.

No sooner had Tess got back down to the kitchen than the emergency bell rang from her room.

"Quick!" she cried. "I bet Bessie's had a fall. She was drawing her curtains when I left her."

We charged upstairs expecting to find her on the floor. Instead she was sitting upright in her chair absolutely stiff with rage, her eyes bulging and her hands gripping the arms of the chair with such force, she was practically lifting herself off the seat.

"What sort of rubbish do you call this when it's at home? If I wanted to eat foreign muck, I'd move to a ruddy foreign country wouldn't I?" She hollered this with such force, I thought she'd explode and I was so taken aback, I just stood there speechless and watched in disbelief as Wanty Wanty turned the whole thing around:

"Keep your hair on! It's a pig's trotters and escargots sauté on a bed of frogs legs and diced sweetbread, garnished with whole cloves of garlic in kipper juice, a famous East End speciality."

He said this slowly, waving his hand in deference over the spaghetti as if it were priceless. Then he pressed his thumb and forefinger together and kissed them with ridiculous exaggeration and threw the kiss in the direction of the ceiling. Already unable to suppress an emerging smile, Bessie sat back in the chair and looked at me,

"What's he on about?" she asked, raising her chin and tilting her head in his direction.

I shrugged my shoulders, barely able to contain myself.

"It's a well known dish, you must have had it loads of times." continued Wanty Wanty convincingly.

"Go on with you, you silly sod." she laughed, as Wanty Wanty carried on in the same vein:

"As any *true* Eastender will tell you, it can be garnished with herring juice, eel juice, or mackerel juice if you prefer. Remember?"

She was laughing so much now, she was having serious trouble keeping her teeth in.

"Don't be so daft, just get me a sandwich or something, long as it's English." she spluttered, wiping her eyes with the napkin.

Wanty Wanty had picked up the tray and was holding the door open for me and as I passed him he was whistling 'Arrivederci Roma'.

One of the meals we eventually did get down to a fine art was our Sunday roast, which we served on bank holidays as well. I don't think we ever came across an elderly person who didn't love a traditional English roast, so its success was practically guaranteed, nevertheless some vital adjustments had to be made because, when we were newcomers to the business we rotated different meats over five weeks to make the compulsory menus look suitably varied, as in: Sunday, week one: roast beef; week two: roast pork; week three: roast lamb; week four: roast chicken; week five: roast turkey. But it wasn't long before we cottoned on that the chicken and the turkey were popular whereas the other meats, however fresh or well cooked, were always too tough and never got eaten. All the trimmings were polished off, but the meat invariably came back half chewed on the plates. It was then that Wanty Wanty had a brain wave.

When it was his turn to do the shopping one particular week, instead of the beef on the menu, he came back with a Bernard Mathews Turkey Breast Joint. Shaped into a roll and unrecognisable as meat of any kind, it had the added bonus of not having to be defrosted before being cooked.

"What we'll do," he explained "is cook it first, then carve it lengthwise into nice thin, different sized slices, cover it in dark gravy, put it back in the oven for a while to soak up the colour, serve it with Yorkshire puddings and horseradish sauce and say it's beef."

Well, we didn't actually lie, we went round to each resident with a jar of sauce and asked:

"Would you like some horseradish with your beef?"

And the outcome was staggering:

"I haven't been able to eat beef for years," remarked Mrs W "but that was so tender, it melted in your mouth."

"Lovely tender beef" added the Captain, who was a man of very few words.

"I bet you've got a good butcher, you need a good butcher, I've cooked a few meals in my time, so I should know, that was jolly good meat, jolly good meat." observed Florence.

Spurred on by this success, when it came to passing it off as pork, Wanty Wanty confidently carved it into slightly thicker slices, made a lighter coloured gravy and served it with apple sauce. Turning it into lamb only required him to marinate it in mint gravy and changing it into chicken just needed the addition of some sage and onion stuffing. Abracadabra!

Chapter 15

When Tess first started working in the rest home she was about thirteen and still at school wanting to earn some extra pocket money. She did Sundays and bank holidays and was allocated housekeeping and catering tasks only. She'd always been domesticated, but for somebody so young she was really capable and responsible, learning the tray system, the various likes and dislikes as well as Wanty Wanty's magic cooking techniques without any difficulty.

Before too long we were able to employ her best friend Liz to work alongside her and they eventually became an indomitable team proficient enough to be left in charge of the kitchen from 10am until 6pm, which gave Wanty Wanty and me a nice easy day.

Unfortunately Liz was on holiday with her parents that particular Easter, so Tess was working in the kitchen on her own, nevertheless she made and served all the hot drinks, kept the whole place clean and tidy and produced a delicious roast something or other.

To set up our own quality control department, at lunch we always ate the same food we made for the residents, as did any visiting friends or relations. This ensured that standards were maintained and we couldn't fault Tess's brilliant efforts that day. Neither could Miss Older, who said it was the best roast whatever it was we said it was, she'd had in a very long time!

Apart from quality control, our lunchtimes also doubled up as staff meetings and discussions relating to the running of the home, so as soon as we finished serving the residents, we sat down to have our lunch and check the list of things to do.

Having put calcium tablets on the shopping list and given Miss Older one of Florence's for the time being (yet another breach of some regulation or other) we were able to tick off several items. Then Wanty Wanty was elected to talk to Mrs Swain about her temporary room-mate, Tess to put away Mrs W's things and change her bed and myself to go over to the bungalow. None of this of course, before serving coffees, clearing away, washing up and setting the many trays for afternoon tea and suppers, details of which I hardly need to go into again.

This only left the paper work, which could be done during supper, serving tea with Mrs Swain, which wasn't really an extra job, and getting in touch with her G.P., which we couldn't do until after Easter. So I wrote the GP's name in the diary for Tuesday and threw the list away.

It was all going so well.

In the bungalow, Miss Older's things were exactly where she said they'd be, as was the monogrammed vintage leather suitcase inherited from her father, and it didn't take long for me to pack enough clothing to see her through the week and I was back in the rest home in less than half an hour.

In room three, Wanty Wanty was helping Tess to make the bed, having already introduced Mrs Swain and Miss Older.

"You must be the daft old codger from next door." Mrs Swain had said to everybody's surprise. "How do you do? Don't worry, I'm a daft old codger as well!"

" I think I'm going to feel at home here," shouted Miss Older.

I unpacked and Tess found a home for things while they chatted. Wanty Wanty did nothing in particular, except jolly things along a bit and all of a sudden it was three o'clock. Time to put the kettle on and do another 'loo run'.

We went off in our usual directions: Tess to the kitchen, Wanty Wanty upstairs and me to coax Louise out of her chair. So far, so good.

"Louise," I said in my sweetest voice "would you come upstairs to look at some flowers and tell me what they are? Nobody else seems to know."

"Yes of course. I used to be a florist, you know."

"I told them you'd know." I said, rather pleased with this spontaneous new ploy of mine. There really was a vase of flowers on the sideboard upstairs, but I was banking on her forgetting what I'd said by the time we got there.

"I used to get fresh flowers from Covent Garden market." she continued, as we made our way to the chair lift. "Do you know it?"

If she said this once, she said it a thousand times. It was quite the strangest thing. Each time, she would say it with a proud freshness, as if saying it for the very first time and as comical as it was, it was equally as endearing. Thinking up something new for a reply was the tricky bit, but as luck would have it on this occasion, before I could do so, the emergency bell rang diverting her attention.

This was the moment things started to get a bit frantic.

"It's Mrs Morris, I think she's had another stroke," mouthed Wanty Wanty, leaning over the banister on the top landing. Louise was concentrating on keeping the starter button on the control panel depressed as the chair lift travelled up the stairs and she didn't notice me walk up past her to open the bathroom door wide.

"There you are." I said. "Will you need any help?"

"I can manage, thank you."

She wandered in as I'd hoped and I followed Wanty Wanty into room six where Edith was having one of her sweetness and smiles moments and was talking to herself in a sing-song sort of voice:

"Look at that beautiful sunshine streaming through the window and the sky is so blue, not a cloud to be seen." Wanty Wanty was holding Mrs Morris' hand with a really worried expression on his face, she in turn was looking up at him all flushed, her eyes wide and watery.

"GRLURR CKLOGEEK GLUCK" she was saying, dribbling a little on the left side of her mouth.

"She's talking gibberish," explained Wanty Wanty helpfully. I looked at Mrs Morris and tried to assess her condition. She appeared too alert somehow and more distressed than I imagined a stroke victim might be. I was so deep in thought that the doorbell suddenly ringing made me jump out of my skin. Wanty Wanty and I looked at each-other, both knowing that this signalled the return of the Captain, which always required Wanty Wanty's immediate attention, being that he invariably needed the toilet urgently upon his return.

"You go." I said

"I'll go," said Wanty Wanty simultaneously.

The pressure was really on now, as Louise would need help in a minute and both Miss Older and Mrs Swain still had to go to the loo before Tess served afternoon tea. But I knew it was important to concentrate on one thing at a time and stay calm, so I took hold of Mrs Morris' hand.

"Now let's see, what are you trying to tell us, I wonder." I said.

" GRLURR CKLOGEEK GLUCK." she repeated a few times with increasing urgency pointing to her mouth. I stood there feeling quite useless for a while and all of a sudden I grasped what it was she was trying to say. *The toffee's stuck*, that's what it was! I took control of the situation. I held her chin with one hand, just as I'd done with Tess when she was little, and I investigated her mouth with the forefinger of the other.

She had both upper and lower dentures and they tried to sever my finger in half, but the hand holding her chin gained the upper hand (if you'll pardon the pun) and was able to save the day. What the forefinger found was a large mass of well-chewed toffee, which was stuck to the roof of her mouth. The more she'd tried to dislodge it with her tongue, the more her dentures had moved and the more paralysed her mouth had become, hence the gibberish. Mrs Morris laughed loudly.

"Thank the Lord!" she sighed, gaining control of the toffee. "I thought I'd never get through to you."

"You gave the boss a nasty shock," I said. "Are you alright now?"

"I think so." she replied, still laughing. "Poor Henty. Well I call him Henty, that's not his name, I know....Cuthbert....no that's not it....Bertrand....no, no, no, silly me.... I'll never get it right. Anyway he did look worried, didn't he?"

Louise was still in the bathroom at this point and, as I walked towards the closed door, Wanty Wanty reached the top of the stairs with the Captain. He realised in an instant that the bathroom was occupied, otherwise the door would have been open, so he steered him in the direction of the separate loo, which was located on the top landing next to room six. Like passing ships in the night, we got on with our respective tasks, but I couldn't help noticing that it was probably too late for the Captain, who was dancing up and down on the spot.

It now really seemed as though we were spiralling out of control.

I knocked on the bathroom door.

"Are you OK Louise?"

"Come in" she called out.

A fairly familiar scene presented itself when I walked in. She was standing at the sink looking at herself in the mirror. The paper on the loo roll holder was unwound to floor level, the hand towel was hanging over the bath taps, which were both turned on full and she was holding her handbag open, the contents of which were lined up on the bath surround. Used napkins, a faded photo or two, some hairgrips, newspaper cuttings, an old brooch with no pin in the back, an empty glasses case, part of a powder compact and a paper back with no front cover.

"Shall I put these back in your bag?" I asked, turning the taps off.

"If you don't mind" she replied politely. "I was looking for some lipstick."

I placed the items in the open compartment of her bag.

"Perhaps it's in the other compartment." I suggested and she grabbed the handbag with one unexpected defiant movement and held it close to her chest.

"I've already looked in there!" she blurted out unnecessarily.

"I expect it'll be on your dressing table then" I remarked condescendingly, backing away from both her and the now suspicious bag.

She followed me out of the bathroom and I helped her on to the chair lift, reminding her which button to press. I went back to clean the seat and tidy up.

"The Captain'll have to have a bath," announced Wanty Wanty appearing in the doorway. "What's happening with Mrs Morris?"

"She's fine. She got toffee stuck, that's all."

"You're joking!"

We walked down the stairs together, laughing at the absurdity of it all and he went off to get some things from the Captain's room, during which time I got Mrs Swain to the bathroom and back. Then he got the Captain out of the little loo and into the bathroom, so I took Miss Older to the little loo and got her back down in time for tea and, blow me down, the emergency bell in room six only rang again. Up I went yet another time and as I got closer to the room, I could hear Mrs Morris saying,

"Get the hook. Get the hook!"

Or more accurately in gibberish:

"GLEH GKLUH KHLOOK, GLEH GKLUH KHLOOK."

"What does she mean? I can't understand what she wants" Wanty Wanty was getting exasperated.

"Get the hook. She's saying 'Get the hook'" I explained calmly, holding up my hooked forefinger and wiggling it at him annoyingly.

Then I swung into action with its toffee removing function. I had the presence of mind not to leave the toffee in her mouth this time, putting it straight in the bin instead. I left them both laughing and Wanty Wanty was threatening her with detention if he ever caught her eating toffee again.

At last everything was back to normal.

Chapter 16

Downstairs, Tess had already started serving the teas. The familiar chinking of cups and the spicy aroma of toasted hot cross buns filled me with a sense of well being as well as a kind of normality, in addition to which the thought of my tea break with some much needed 'non-contact time' and a desperately needed cigarette soothed my frazzled spirits, as I made my way back to the kitchen.

Passing room three, I noticed that Mrs Swain and Miss Older already had their tea and I hadn't passed Tess on my way down. This was odd, because everything was usually served in room order and room four was upstairs. Tess must have had to go back, I reasoned. Then I heard Louise's raised voice as I passed room one:

"How dare you call me names! It's dumb insolence. I'll report you to the manager."

And Tess's apologetic reply:

"No, no, you don't understand, I didn't call you a name. Punk is a kind of fashion."

I knocked on the door, interrupting:

"Is everything alright?"

I got the shock of my life when I saw Louise. There she was, sitting beautifully poised as always, her back straight, her feet neatly placed together and hands clasped in her lap like a real English lady, with the most gruesome black kohl pencil smeared all over her mouth, a garish bright red lipstick smudged round her eyes and big patches of pure white powder plastered all over her face.

Tess had been under the impression that Louise was upstairs and had placed her tea and bun with the Captain's in the lounge. On her way to serve teas in room three, she'd heard Louise moving about, so had gone back to room one to invite her to tea.

"Goodness me, what on earth have you done to your face?" was her instinctive reaction, which she realised immediately was the wrong thing to say because of the thunderous look she got back from Louise.

"I'll bring your tea into your room, shall I?" she added, quickly changing the subject.

Returning with the tea, she made things worse by trying to make them better:

"Actually, it's quite cool. You look a bit like a Punk."

And that's when I'd heard Louise's raised and very angry voice.

As fond of Louise as we were, she wasn't really a very nice person. She had absolutely no sense of humour, she had a superior attitude and was often bossy and defensive. She could be difficult at times due to her senility, which was forgivable, but you could tell she'd never liked young attractive girls, for example and treated Tess and Liz as if they were the 'hired help', which made her unpopular with everybody. The only way to diffuse the difficult situations she seemed to regularly cause was to pretend she hadn't done anything wrong and make her feel like a special client, which is what I had to do now, in spite of the fact that she clearly hadn't had any reason to get so cross.

"Ah, there you are Louise, you're booked in for hairdressing and beauty therapy this afternoon, I'll tell them you're ready." I said, giving Tess the opportunity to get out of the room.

"Thank you!" she replied, regaining her composure.

Louise loved being pampered. It made her feel important and I knew this was the only way we were going to be able to get her back to normal.

I joined Tess in the corridor. It was impossible not to laugh and difficult to work out why Louise would have made herself look so weird.

"Dad'll have to see it, or he won't believe us, will he?" said Tess conspiratorially.

I informed her that Wanty Wanty was upstairs giving the Captain a bath and that she could go and tell him while I wasted a bit of time setting Louise's hair first. She covered the

Captain's tea and went off with the tray, while I got a bag of make-up remover, rollers etc, before going back to Louise.

"Now then Madame." I said. "I'll set your hair while you're having your tea, if that's alright."

"I always order tea while I'm having my hair done." she informed me rather pompously, holding the cup and saucer up together.

She'd already made a great black lip mark on the cup, but was continuing to drink imperviously. I wondered momentarily whether swallowing mouthfuls of kohl-laden tea might be harmful in any way, but didn't dare upset the apple cart and remained silent, while I sprayed the sections of hair with setting lotion and wound them round the rollers.

Before too long, Wanty Wanty knocked on the door and came in with the excuse of collecting the empties. He left the room in silence, not before glancing knowingly at me with raised eyebrows and pursed lips.

Louise was so impressed with the various bottles of skin-care products that she didn't ask any questions and I got her back to normal in no time at all with some pink lipstick and blusher and I handed her a large magnifying mirror to look at the result.

There was no doubt she must have been an extremely attractive woman in her youth and there were times I truly felt for her and understood her sense of loss. Anyway, while she was admiring her reflection, I packed my equipment away together with her black kohl pencil and red lipstick in such a flurry of activity that she didn't notice I'd taken them, but there was no way of sneaking off with the handbag because it was hanging on the arm of the chair, right there where she was sitting. A more elaborate plan was going to be needed for that!

By the time the Captain was dressed and back downstairs, his tea and bun had gone cold and Wanty Wanty had to go and make him a fresh lot. Not one to be kept waiting, though, the Captain headed out to the garden.

"Bring it out on the deck, would you old chap" he ordered, as if he were still in the Royal Navy.

Whatever the weather, the Captain was outside, pacing up and down and smoking. He was never still. He'd sit on a bench for a moment or two, then he'd be up again, and if he wasn't pacing or smoking, he was swaying from side to side with his hands behind his back, as if standing on the bridge of his ship. He had the front door key on a string round his neck, so he could come and go as he wanted to.

His favourite tipple was Special Brew, which was rationed to two cans a day, one before lunch and one before supper and he was always on time for these, whereas mealtimes themselves were an inconvenient necessity and more often than not, one of us would have to go and fetch him. He would then, quite literally, sit down, eat the food, as if performing a duty and leave the table to go back outside. He was such a gentleman though and much loved by everybody. Wanty Wanty was particularly fond of him and developed a special bond, the Captain being especially happy when Wanty Wanty found time to join him for a Special Brew before supper.

Naturally, Wanty Wanty made out it was purely out of a sense of duty that he was obliged to keep his own supply of Special Brew and naturally we all believed him.

Apparently, the Captain had been on his own for several years before coming to the rest home, but his family never spoke about his wife or what happened to her, they only spoke about what happened to him and why they had all reluctantly agreed that he needed full time care.

The story went something like this:

He'd moved into the annexe of his daughter's house so that he could maintain his independence with a little help. She would, for example, organize his shopping, make his meals, ensure all his bills were paid, etc. and the arrangement worked well for several years.

One day the Captain's daughter arrived home from work and found him sitting in his armchair crying.

"Oh Daddy, darling, whatever is the matter?"

"It's Skipper," replied the Captain, sniffing loudly. "I went to the Post Office this morning to get some stamps and when I came out, I untied his lead and he just seemed to crumble to the ground. He could hardly stand let alone walk, bless him, and I picked him up and carried him all the way to the vet. Oh, it's heartbreaking, the vet said he was a very old dog with serious arthritic joints and was in so much pain that the kindest thing would be to put him down. What a decision! I couldn't bear to be parted from the poor creature, but I knew it was the right thing to do and now Skipper is no longer with us."

"But Daddy," said the daughter "Skipper died five years ago!"

The Captain was dumbfounded. "Are you sure?" he mumbled. The vet confirmed that the Captain had indeed taken a dog fitting exactly the same description of the late Skipper into the surgery that same afternoon, but they never found out whom it belonged to.

The sad thing for the Captain was that he'd grieved the loss of Skipper the first time and now he was going to have to do it all over again.

The sad thing for his daughter was the realization that she could no longer leave him on his own. Not only had he suffered a serious lapse of memory, he was still wearing his pyjamas under his clothing, he'd forgotten to eat his lunch and afternoon snack and he'd polished off more than twice his allowance of Special Brew into the bargain!

In the end, he was more than happy to move into the rest home, as we were only down the road and he was able to walk to his daughter's house, see the same faces, find his way around and go to the same shops, including the Post Office.

Luckily, there was no repeat of the dog incident, but we'll never know whether that was purely because nobody else in the neighbourhood had a dog like Skipper!

Chapter 17

It was nearly quarter to five before we were able to sit down for our tea break. My legs were throbbing, my feet were aching and I could easily have sat and smoked a whole packet of cigarettes, never mind the one I was desperate for.

Thank God it was a bank holiday and Tess was on duty, otherwise we'd have had to miss the break altogether and start getting supper ready.

Supper was served at half past five and, on Sundays and bank holidays, consisted of a round of sandwiches, usually smoked salmon or prawn mayonnaise, with a salad garnish (purely for decoration and not usually eaten) and a few crisps. Afterwards we offered some fruit or a piece of cake. This was easy enough for one of us to manage, as everything could be prepared, plated and covered about half an hour before serving, whereas weekday suppers were mostly hot meals and had to be served as soon as they were plated, which was a little more tricky for one person to accomplish without a major drama.

Having said that, we were very particular about our sandwiches. We used medium sliced wholemeal bread, spread generously with real English butter right to the edges, none of that measly scraping of margarine nonsense, and the filling had to be thick enough to be seen clearly between the two slices and then the crusts had to be cut off.

All the residents loved our sandwiches and, like our Sunday roasts, their success was guaranteed. Indeed Miss Older couldn't have arrived on a better day in terms of the menu and, had we been trying to convince her of the benefits of residential care, we'd have won hands down.

It wasn't just the food, though. Had she come on a Tuesday, Wanty Wanty wouldn't have been on duty. Had she come on a Wednesday, I wouldn't have been on duty and had it not been a bank holiday, Tess wouldn't have been on duty. But she happened to come to us when all three of us were together, with the family atmosphere at its best. Not only that, but there was an empty bed to boot. The chances of all these things coming together on the very same day as Miss Older getting into her predicament were about a million to one and when I went to sit with her to have the promised cigarette after supper, she told me precisely that.

She thanked me I don't know how many times and said that this had been her lucky day. She told me she'd long since been concerned about what she might do when she became 'old and decrepit', especially as she had no family, but she'd been convinced that we were the kind of people who'd advise her and help her, adding that she'd always been a good judge of character.

We stubbed our cigarettes out and walked along the hall to room three. I drew the curtain across the room and got both her and Mrs Swain to sit on their respective beds, which had been turned down in the usual way when the empty supper trays were collected. I put their meal trolleys in front of them with a bowl of hot water each, their flannels, towels and toiletries within easy reach and left them to have a wash while I put Steradent in their tooth boxes. Then I helped them into their nightdresses. Mrs Swain knew the system well and could manage most tasks by herself. Miss Older's broken arm made it impossible for her, but she tried her very best to make it easy for me to help.

Finally, when I took her shoes and stockings off, I realised why she'd been walking oddly and possibly why she'd lost her balance and fallen over in the first place. Her toenails were so long that they'd started to curl over at the ends like a bird of prey. I'd never seen anything like it. They were truly an inch long or maybe more.

"Good heavens!" I exclaimed. "When was the last time these were cut?"

"I can't see that far down," she replied, laughing. "Even if I could, I wouldn't be able to reach them!"

Chapter 18

With the exception of Edith, who was incontinent, all the residents had a commode next to their bed at night.

Leaving an elderly person to get up in the middle of the night, put a dressing gown on, negotiate the famous one-hour fire doors, walk up the corridor or up the stairs, find the toilet and get back into their own bed was asking for trouble and taking the phrase 'responsible risk taking' way too far.

It was essential therefore to teach each resident a system of using the commode safely, tailored to his or her individual needs. Even Mrs Swain was independent during the night and to be honest, had she not been, it may well have been very difficult for us to accept her. Small family run homes, such as ours couldn't afford the luxury of employing night staff and, although it was acceptable for owners living on the premises to be on call for emergencies, it was not permissible for them to have regular night duties.

Anyway, before tucking Miss Older into bed, I went through a procedure, which I thought was best for her.

Lying in Mrs W's bed, the dividing curtain was on her left, the bedside table on her right. I put the commode on her right facing the bed, about a foot away with the arms parallel to the bedside table, where I placed her torch and a box of tissues. I suggested she switch the torch on first, sit herself up and swing her legs round so as to face the commode, take the lid off and place it on the floor under the commode then cross her left hand over to the left arm of the commode, using it to lean on while standing up. Once in the standing position, turn around to face the bed, get her nightdress up, again with the left hand and tuck it under the right arm at elbow point, holding it tight to her body. Still with the left hand, find the left arm of the commode behind and slowly lower herself onto the seat. Afterwards do everything in reverse and put the lid back on. Now what could be easier?

The training session went well and, just to make sure she'd got the hang of it, she practised it two or three times and Mrs Swain decided it would be very helpful if she sang a little song, so, while Miss Older was bellowing out in her usual loud voice,

"First the torch, then sit up, swing the legs round, lid off, left hand out…"

Mrs Swain was singing quietly,

"You put your left hand in, your left hand out, in out, in out, you shake it all about…"

Chapter 19

We always tried to get those who needed a lot of help to get ready for bed all done by about 7pm when we were supposed to have finished what we called 'active duty'. After that, apart from doing the rounds at 10.30pm, going through the lock up procedure and of course being on call through the night, our working day was over.

In the evening, Tess was always busy with homework, singing lessons or rehearsals, so we'd put some music on and pour ourselves a large well-earned drink and, as fully committed members of the Mutual Admiration Society, we'd congratulate each other on our achievements of the day. This was an excellent way of keeping our spirits up and injecting the enthusiasm we needed to tackle the same tasks the following day. In any case, it was impossible to go out together in the evening to unwind, because we seriously couldn't afford to employ two qualified people to take our place, as was required by law. Friends and family quickly learned not to invite us out and to drop by instead and, on those occasions we'd put The Mutual Admiration Society on hold and keep them amused with all the stories about our business venture.

One of our favourite stories was the one about the time we approached our local bank manager for a business loan to buy the failing rest home.

We'd saved a decent deposit and done our homework by viewing a good cross section of small homes for sale, finding out what fees on average were being charged and what facilities and standards were on offer. We'd even been to view some vacancies being advertised, pretending to be looking for a home for an elderly relative. We then prepared a detailed business plan with the help of a book from the library.

We outlined our philosophy and principles of care as well as our intention to change the home's name and our ideas on how we intended to promote it in order to maintain high occupancy levels. Then we enclosed forecast figures for the first two years. Our branch manager was impressed with our presentation and referred us to the head office's department for business loans where the manager of the 'Residential Care Homes Sector' was located and an interview was duly set up.

A copy of our business plan had to be sent ten days in advance of our interview and the head office was a two hour journey from where we lived, so on the day of the interview, as we hadn't received a rejection in the post, we were quietly confident going into the building, looking suitably smart and businesslike. But as soon as we walked into the office, we both knew we'd been rejected by the pompous and supercilious smirk on the manager's fat pretentious face. He could have simply written a polite letter of refusal and saved us the journey as well as the trouble of us both getting the day off work, but oh no, he actually took great pleasure in us being present while he rubbished everything we'd written. In particular, he was absolutely adamant that the weekly fee we proposed to charge was way in excess of the local average, mentioning the name of a home he was familiar with, which not only charged a good deal less, but also had it's own bus providing regular outings for the residents.

Regular bus outings? We'd clearly stated that our intention was to provide a lifestyle which as closely as possible resembled that of being in ones own home with the attention focused on the individual. Herding people onto a bus for outings? I don't think so!

We later discovered that the home in question was registered for thirty residents, the antithesis of our basic philosophy for quality of care and that the social security benefit for people in 'Residential Care' was twenty-five pounds more than our proposed fee. What a wally!

Anyway he spent the rest of the interview bragging about his extensive experience and expertise and told us in no uncertain terms that we didn't have a hope in hell of succeeding in this line of business. There was no apology and absolutely no sympathy when our faces dropped in disappointment.

Eventually, we closed our accounts and moved to a different bank. Then we found a private financial backer who believed in us.

Two years later, when the business was thriving with an excellent reputation, a waiting list and a perfectly decent annual turnover, we received a letter from our old bank. It was a stock circular giving established rest homes the opportunity to re-finance with an amazing special low interest offer. Not only that, but a personal home visit was proposed by an expert in the care home business, who would discuss the matter fully with free financial advice and no obligation.

Anybody in their right mind with only the slightest business acumen would have looked into any re-financing offer in the hope of reducing costs, but guess what we decided to do? We decided to be completely childish and unprofessional and we phoned to make an appointment for the sole purpose of telling our old bank where to stick its money. We couldn't be sure that the 'expert' referred to in the letter would be the same manager who'd rejected us, but any small satisfaction was worth having.

On the allotted day Wanty Wanty answered the door and recognized him immediately. Yes, it was the very same bloke! Oh joy! Oh happy day! Thank you God!

Wanty Wanty let him in, shaking his hand firmly and smiling broadly. Then he led him along the hall slowly, pausing to check on Mrs Swain in room three, so as to give him plenty of time to take in the chairlift and the plush new carpets. He showed him through to the lounge, where the residents were listening to classical music on the radio and he opened the door to the kitchen letting him go first. I was dispensing tablets from the medicine cabinet and looked up.

I greeted the instantly recognizable fat face politely, I offered him a cup of tea or coffee and I directed him to the seat at the head of the table, which gave him a comprehensive view of the absolutely spotless, brand new kitchen.

We let him do his sales patter, his slick sales pitch and we showed him the excellent state of our annual accounts. He in turn showed no sign of recognizing us and had no recollection of our names or the previous name of the home.

Then Wanty Wanty reminded him who we were and what he'd said to us on that momentous occasion, adding that under the circumstances, we couldn't be confident of any advice he might give and in any case we were very unlikely to put business his way.

Trying his best not to look phased, he mumbled something about how rare it was for him to be proven wrong, but his haughty grin was wiped straight off his horrible face.

Oh sweet vengeance! We both revelled in it for ages and still do, in case you hadn't noticed.

Chapter 20

Now where was I? Ah yes, Good Friday, early evening, drink in hand, mutual admiration society meeting over. While Wanty Wanty made our dinner, I got the paper work done for Miss Older.

I took out a temporary admissions card from the index box to fill in with her personal details and, as was the norm for all residents, I wrote her name on a new exercise book to be used to explain the circumstances of her admission, devise an appropriate care-plan and record any important events or changes in her condition or needs.

I filled in the admissions card using the details I got from her before lunch, with the exception of her doctor's telephone number, which she didn't have with her. I couldn't find a Dr J.R. Griffiths listed in the directory, so I left the card on the desk diary to complete at a later date, as well as a reminder to call the chiropodist for an urgent appointment. Then I put the exercise book together with her medical card in the folder we'd taken out earlier.

Over dinner we talked about the recent 1984 Act of Parliament and what we'd have to do in order to comply with all the new regulations.

Firstly we'd need to produce a document setting out our 'terms and conditions of residence', which all 'clients' would have to sign before moving in, and to find out whether we would need a solicitor for such a thing. Then we'd have to get our 'aims and objectives' formally documented as well as a brochure detailing the location, the facilities and layout of the home. We'd need to decide which one of us would attend the first aid course, which one the basic health and hygiene course and we'd have to work out how the hell we were going to be able to afford it all.

Amongst all the jargon sent to us, we couldn't see anything about the status of temporary residents or whether the terms and conditions of residence would apply to them as well, so there was yet another item to put in the desk diary.

A particular bone of contention for small homeowners was the proposed new regulation about the ratio of double occupancy rooms permitted. This was going to be strictly one in ten, in other words all those registered for less than ten residents would be allowed single rooms only. How were they supposed to survive? In fact, how the bloody hell were WE supposed to survive?

We discussed how, prior to the act, people like ourselves all over the country had bought registered rest homes with double rooms in good faith, having obtained financial backing on the strength of a certain number of potential clients. To think that the government could suddenly implement such sweeping changes was crazy. What about the viability of all those businesses? What about the security of tenure for all those elderly people? No, we convinced ourselves, they wouldn't get away with it. New builds maybe, but not established homes, it simply couldn't happen. What about people who actually wanted a double room? What would become of Mrs Swain, who was relieved to find a sharing room in a small rest home at a fee she could afford as opposed to a nursing home at a fee which would see her penniless long before she died? Neither was it very clear what would happen to her in the meantime. Mrs W was in the same situation. Presumably we'd have to wait until they both died before turning room three into two singles. The same would apply to number six, Edith and Mrs Morris' room. We'd have to get stud walls built down the middle of both rooms and end up with four long narrow prison cells with half windows in each. Yuck! We'd seen so many during our research days, apart from which, the prospect of any more building work just when we'd got the place sorted, filled us with dread.

We discussed my favoured option of getting plans drawn up professionally by Wanty Wanty's architect brother for the conversion of both rooms and to have them ready to show the inspector, but to then keep stalling with excuses such as lack of funding, urgent admissions, illness and so on.

Needless to say, this wasn't really our style. In reality, our bottle of wine was emptying fast and we were beginning to talk a load of old twaddle! Still, it kept us entertained until lockup, bath and bedtime.

Chapter 21

"She hasn't made a single sound all night long," whispered Mrs Swain when I served early morning tea on Saturday. "Actually, I think she might be dead."

" Must you be so blunt?" I whispered back while helping her into her luxurious cream cashmere bed jacket.

"Dying is very blunt" she retorted. "One minute you're breathing, then you're not." We both laughed quietly and I guided her hand to the handle on her cup.

"There," I said "drink your tea, it'll stop you talking!"

"IS THAT YOU SONEEA?" bellowed Miss Older suddenly from the other side of the curtain, frightening the life out of us both and causing me to spill her tea into the saucer.

"Good morning Madame" I said and poured it back into the cup before taking it round to her.

"We though you were dead." added Mrs Swain, luckily at the same time as Miss Older said:

"Oooh, how lovely! I've never had a cup of tea brought to me in bed."

"What, not one single knight in shining armour to bring you a cup of tea in the morning?" enquired Mrs Swain, digging for details. Miss Older looked up at me.

"What did she say?"

I translated the bit about the knight and the tea into louder English and wrapped her pale blue hand knitted shawl round her shoulders.

"My knight in shining armour never came back from the war, dear." she replied. "I knew I couldn't replace him, so I didn't bother trying."

She wasn't looking for sympathy, just stating a fact. Mrs Swain understood this instinctively and decided to veer away from the topic of lost loves.

"How did you manage on your own?"

"She wants to know how you managed on your own." I said automatically.

"Quite well really, dear. I had a good job in the Civil Service and I bought my own bungalow. I liked work. It gave me independence you know. And a good pension! What about you dear?"

"I married my knight and brought up our two sons. Three full time jobs if you ask me. Without the decent pension either!"

"I see dear."

Mrs Swain knew she hadn't heard a word by the unconvincing tone of her voice.

"We make a right old pair, don't we?" she laughed. " She's lost her hearing, I've lost my sight and we've both lost our teeth!"

"Well at least you haven't lost your marbles." I told her as I drew the curtains and opened a window."

"That would be really careless!" she replied with a chuckle. While I rinsed both sets of dentures and placed them back into their respective boxes I glanced in Miss Older's direction and caught her telling me in sign language that she hadn't heard a thing and didn't want to give the impression she was being rude. I brought her up to speed when I handed over her dentures in the box. She laughed and shouted back to Mrs Swain:

"We haven't lost our sense of humour either, that would be even more careless, wouldn't it dear?"

Mrs Swain smiled broadly, happy to find somebody on her wavelength and I handed over her top denture first, then the bottom one, in the usual way.

I was on automatic pilot and hardly aware of handling the false teeth, which in the early days would have made me feel positively sick, especially first thing in the morning. Wanty Wanty was the same, but we couldn't afford to be squeamish and just had to get used to it.

Mrs W was the only resident with teeth of her own, not very many I admit, but enough to chew her food adequately and Edith had no teeth at all, either real or false. Everybody else had dentures or partial dentures and Florence was the only one capable of looking after them. The others would either forget to remove them, so they'd fall out of their own accord in the middle of the night and you'd have to hunt through the bedclothes to look for them in the morning, or they'd stick them straight in to soak, so you'd find them in a murky soup with nasty bits of yesterday's supper floating about. Frankly, mornings were more pleasant without either scenario and it was in our best interests to get used to cleaning them ourselves.

Actually, we had some comical experiences with false teeth. I remember a particular time with Bessie, who couldn't get used to having a washbasin in her own room. She'd been in the home for a few years before we came along and had got used to her routine. Every evening after supper she'd get into her nightdress and dressing gown and watch television until bed time, then she'd set her hair in rollers and tie a hair net on before going to the bathroom to do her ablutions.

Long after the washbasins had been installed, while doing the 10.30 rounds, we'd see her going back to her room with her toiletries and remind her about the vanity unit in her room.

"Silly old duffer!" she'd usually say, laughing at herself. "It'll *sink* in one of these days!"

Anyway on the particular night in question, when Wanty Wanty was doing the last rounds while I was doing the lock up, he met Florence coming out of the bathroom on the first landing.

"Good night Florence, is everything all right?"

"Oh yes, thank you for asking... couldn't be better... off to bed now, early to bed, early to rise, always been the same... my folk'll tell you... must get this leg rested, ooh jibber it's punishment... thank God I've got you and your lady wife...good night...God bless you both...good night."

Turning towards the top landing, he then encountered Bessie, who'd obviously found the main bathroom occupied and used the separate loo next to room six. She took a couple of steps forward carrying her denture box, the lid of which had long since become separated and lost, and she came to a halt when she spotted him.

"Here, what's going on? I've never seen nothing like it," she blurted out angrily. "Have a look at this will you. I'm not putting up with it. Not bright blue water, I'm not"

Wanty Wanty examined the contents of the box, which she held out towards him. The liquid was indeed quite blue.

"Where did you get it from, Bessie?"

"Where d'ya think I got it from, for gawd's sake? The *waterspout* in there"

Her telltale eyes were bulging with anger as she pointed to the loo door. It was something she must have done on a regular basis: forgetting about her washbasin and finding the bathroom engaged, she'd held the box inside the toilet and pulled the chain to get some water and on this occasion, I'd put 'Bloo Loo' in the cistern.

"Waterspout? What's that? Anyway, what's wrong with the sink in your own room?" enquired Wanty Wanty patiently.

" Oh no, I forgot all about it again. I must be going daft in me old age," she laughed. "I need some memory powder, that's what I need."

Needless to say, from that moment on, we made a point of getting her teeth done before she got the chance and stopped using Bloo Loo, just in case.

Then there was the special problem with Louise, whose dentures had to be hidden in the recess on top of her wardrobe during the night, completely out of her sight and reach, otherwise she'd get them out again and spill the Steradent solution all over the place. Then she'd either put them in a pocket or in her handbag or she might hide them on the windowsill, behind the curtain, or she'd tidy them away among clothes in a drawer. In the end the final straw was when, oh God, I can't believe I'm telling you this.... she put them in her COMMODE and, wait for it, AFTER using it! Oh no, I think I'm going to be sick!

Chapter 22

All the residents were helped to have a wash and get dressed before breakfast, unless they were going to have a bath, which is what Miss Older opted for on that particular Saturday. She hadn't been able to get into her own bath for years and was looking forward to a proper old soak.

"I didn't notice any lifting apparatus when I was in there yesterday," she remarked when Mrs Swain told her about the magic bath.

"That's because the chair is part of the bath itself and lifts up and out at the press of a button." I explained as best as I could. It was the most exciting design Wanty Wanty and I had found, the only one that didn't look clinical and passed as an ordinary domestic model. It was also the most expensive, but anything less would have made us look hypocritical, given our philosophy and principles of care.

Anyway, the main reason I suggested she had a bath, was to get her feet soaked and hopefully soften those talons, just in case the chiropodist was available for an urgent appointment, so after breakfast I wrapped a plastic bag round her plaster cast and used another to tie up like a sling before lowering her into the warm bubbly water.

I was never a 'compulsive carer'. You know, the typical martyr type, who runs around doing things for other people all the time; whose friends all have problems; whose only way of achieving fulfilment is to look after other people. At least I didn't think I was, because I'd always had a wide circle of friends and lots of interests. Nevertheless, I can't deny a definite sense of satisfaction at the sheer pleasure and gratitude Miss Older expressed to me after wallowing safely in the luxury of a simple bath.

When she was dressed and sitting in her chair, I stopped to reflect on how rewarding it was to bring comfort and a sense of well being to people who couldn't manage the simple tasks of everyday living most of us take for granted.

That's when the doorbell rang.

Wanty Wanty peered round the kitchen door and looked along the length of the house towards room three, where I was standing.

"I'll get it." I called out.

He went back to finish setting up the trays and I went to open the door, which was still locked up and bolted. A surly, stocky policewoman with a butch hairdo was on the doorstep holding a clipboard.

"Morning ma'am. I need to speak to the matron," she said without looking up.

"I'm the matron." I replied. "How can I help?"

"Ah" she said, frowning at her clipboard "Have you got a missing resident?"

"No, I don't think so. In fact, I'm sure we haven't."

"*How* can you be sure? Can you check with your staff please?" she demanded in a bossy voice.

"We haven't got any staff on duty today, just me and my husband" I protested as politely as I could. "Anyway the front door was still bolted."

She looked ahead indifferently.

"Have you done a head-count?"

"Head-count?" I repeated, smiling broadly and trying desperately not to laugh. "We've only got eight residents, they've all had their early morning tea and I can assure you we'd be the first to know if anybody was missing"

"This is no laughing matter, ma'am. We have a very distressed, very confused, very elderly lady in the vehicle and we need to locate her place of residence. It would be helpful if you tried to co-operate"

It crossed my mind that in a minute somebody was going to jump out of the bushes saying: 'Smile, you're on Candid Camera' and after an uncomfortable pause, I decided to take charge.

"Why don't I come and meet her, I'll soon tell you if she's one of ours." I suggested, doing my best not to sound impatient, just in case I was being filmed. But as I walked down the drive towards the police car in the street, I began to feel quite cross and wondered what sort of dumb procedure the daft woman was following and how many hours she was wasting trying to do it. Then I noticed she had a colleague sitting in the driving seat. Blow me down, there were two of them! What a farce!

The poor soul in the back didn't look in the least bit distressed. Neither did she seem confused or even particularly elderly. She was looking out of the window with absolutely no expression on her face and it was instantly obvious to me that she didn't belong in any rest home.

"Does she have a name?" I asked. "And how long has she been sitting in this car?

"She doesn't respond to any questioning," replied the butch hairdo from behind the clipboard. "According to these notes, she was found wandering the streets at zero seven hundred hours."

"That would be approximately three hours then." I stated, gaining confidence. "Has she had anything to drink in that time?"

"Umm, no" the colleague wound down the window.

"Why don't I look after her until you find out where she lives" I proposed, " She could end up sitting in the car all day at this rate!" I opened the back door and crouched down.

"Hello there, would you like a nice cup of tea?"
She stared blankly back at me.

"Come on, it's nice and warm inside we'll get you some breakfast as well."
Then she started to get her legs out and the butch hairdo handed the clipboard to her colleague and helped me to get her out of the car.

"If you would give P.C. Brown your name and telephone number," she said, regaining control of the situation "I'll assist the lady to the front door. We'll contact you as soon as we ascertain her details"

I went along with the plan. I could so easily have told them she wasn't our resident and let them get on with it, but I wanted to show them I knew what I was doing and put the bossy policewoman in her place, or was I a "compulsive carer' after all?

Anyway, quite apart from the fact that I didn't think the lost individual looked much more than say about sixty-five or seventy, you could tell she wasn't as elderly as they thought, because she was perfectly steady on her feet as she walked up the drive with the policewoman. Then, when I joined her she stepped over the threshold unassisted and took her coat off and hung it up effortlessly. The police car drove off.

Under her coat she was wearing a cardigan inside out and on the back collar there was a nametag in bold lettering: DORIS C.

"So, you must be Doris" I said perceptively and I led her to the chairlift to get her straight to the loo. I wasn't going to take any chances. She complied silently and afterwards I settled her into the empty lounge. Nobody was down yet and she looked a sorry sight sitting there all alone with her knee high pop socks showing beneath the hemline of her shrunken, creased up skirt.

"I won't be long Doris," I said. "I'll get you that cup of tea and some hot buttered toast, alright?"
She stared blankly ahead and started humming tunelessly:
"Hmm…hmm…hmm"
It was possible she wasn't even wearing her own clothes and her name wasn't Doris at all, I decided. Apparently it made no difference to her anyway. How absolutely awful! How could this happen? I went into the kitchen.

"Ah there you are" said Wanty Wanty. "Where the bloody hell do you think you've been, while I've been left to carry the full responsibility for the well being of our residents, our daughter and the general running of the whole place single-handedly?"
He was dispensing the tablets and Tess, who was now on duty, raised a hand in front of her mouth pretending to yawn in boredom at his familiar banter. Then she continued getting the coffee tray ready. I told them about Doris.

"Nice one Sonia" remarked Wanty Wanty. "Why don't you invite the whole street? I'm sure we can cram a few more in." He went through to the resident's lounge. Tess and I followed.

"Hello, Doris!" he said cheerfully, holding his hand out as he walked towards her.

"How nice of you to drop in" he took hold of her hand. "How do you do? I'm the boss and this is our daughter Tess."

"I think you'll find I'm the boss" I interrupted.

"The others will be down soon," he added, ignoring me. "If not, Sonia will go and rustle a few more people off the street, so don't you worry"

I swear to God her eyes flickered and the corners of her mouth moved ever so slightly upwards, but she said nothing and we all went back to our duties; Wanty Wanty to coax some resident's down for coffee, Tess to get Doris the promised breakfast before putting the milk on and me to check the diary for things to do.

I decided to try the chiropodist for Miss Older, because I knew he'd come out if he hadn't gone away for Easter. In fact he was a bit of a workaholic and when I told him about Miss Older's talons, he said he could fit her in at three thirty. He told me to soak her feet in hot water with some added baby oil for a good ten minutes before the appointment.

"Quick!" said Tess in a half whisper, her head appearing round the door just as I put the phone down. "Louise's handbag, it's in the lounge."

I followed her out and, sure enough, there it was, the highly suspicious bag sitting on her empty chair. What an opportunity, I wasn't going to need an elaborate plan to purloin it after all. The Captain and Miss Older were busy dunking biscuits into their coffee and Doris was pressing her forefinger onto her plate to collect every last crumb of toast.

"Where's Louise?" I enquired.

"She came out to start with," explained Tess "but when I introduced her to Doris, she took one look at her and said she was going to her room and told me to take her coffee in"

I seized the opportunity and made off with the bag and although the residents were far too busy to notice, I felt like an absolute thief as I walked straight passed Louise's room and upstairs to the bathroom. In the normal way of things, Residents were entitled to their privacy and we always respected their property, but in extraordinary circumstances such as these, exceptions had to be made.

In the unzipped compartment, I found the usual items Louise regularly lined up on her meal trolley or on the bath surround, but when I started to open the zipped compartment, the most putrid stench hit me so hard I flinched in disgust and, in true faint-hearted female mode, I rang the emergency bell for Wanty Wanty!

"Bloody hell! What on earth has she got in there?" he quizzed unhelpfully, when I thrust the bag towards him and he caught a whiff of the fetid odour.

"How should I bloody know?" I replied, equally unhelpfully with my hand clasped over my mouth and nose.

We toyed with the idea of throwing the whole lot in the bin and having done with it, but our curiosity got the better of us and we couldn't be sure there wasn't anything of value in there, so I reached under the sink for some rubber gloves and…handed them to Wanty Wanty! Then we both started laughing, like a couple of school children. I held the bag open, turning my head to one side and Wanty Wanty put the gloves on. One by one, he pulled out dozens of little parcels wrapped in loo paper, tissues or napkins, which were stuffed tightly together and he placed them on the windowsill and, after taking a deep breath, he started to unravel them.

He found a quarter of a prawn sandwich, four Brussels sprouts, some hairpins, a spoonful of spinach, half a sausage roll, a bit of scone with what was once jam and cream, a wodge of loo paper, a garibaldi biscuit, some part-chewed mackerel, a slice of something neither of us could positively identify, three safety pins, some pickled onions, a mouthful of treacle tart with a trace of custard and, perhaps the oddest thing of all, a fossilized eight ounce packet of Anchor butter.

And so it went on and just when we were about to give up and throw the rest away Wanty Wanty came across a ten pound note all folded up round a Steradent tablet, so we had to see it through to the bitter end. Amongst other smelly items of rotting food, we eventually found a total of twenty-eight pounds fifty as well as the wedding ring Louise had long since reported missing, or more accurately, stolen and we were glad we'd persevered with it.

We decided to tell her all about it and to advise her that in future we were going to have to routinely go through her bag. She seemed to be quite pleased about this, especially when we handed her the money and the wedding ring.

While all this was going on, P.C. Brown telephoned and told Tess that the Matron of a local E.M.I. home (that's Elderly Mentally Infirm) had reported Doris missing, so could we please take her back there at our earliest convenience. Bloody cheek.

I wasted a great deal of time trying to phone the local police station, where in the end nobody knew anything about the incident. Then I waited on the line for ages to speak to the matron of the home in question, who was busy with a 'client' and eventually she informed me that she wasn't allowed to leave the premises whilst on duty and that it would be very helpful if I would kindly take her there. It was OK apparently for *me* to leave *our* premises, but I wasn't going to waste any more time and I bit the bullet and got Doris belted up in the passenger seat of the car. The Captain asked, as he always did, whether he could come along for the ride.

"Clunk, click every trip" he said, as he got in the back and fastened himself in.

I drove the short distance to the home and stopped the car right outside the main entrance of the single storey council building. I rang the doorbell and Doris and I stood looking through the glass door for a considerable length of time before a member of staff approached. Bursting out of the dreaded nylon overall, lime green of all colours, she took a while to tap her code into the security system before the lock was released and I wondered how on earth Doris had managed it during her escape. She opened the door, leaned forward and took hold of Doris' hand.

"Ah, there you are. Who's a naughty girl then? In you come, Doris."

The door clicked shut behind them, leaving me on the doorstep as if I didn't exist and I stood there in disbelief, watching them walk away down the corridor and out of sight. I considered ringing the bell again and giving somebody a piece of my mind, then I considered kicking the door, but the Captain had joined me and was standing with his hands behind his back swaying in the usual way, so I thought it best to beat a hasty retreat.

"Do you want to sit in the front?" I asked, diverting his attention.

"Good idea!" he replied and we both got in the car.

I turned the car round, wishing I'd brought my cigarettes with me.

"Look!" said the Captain as we drove back past the entrance. "She's come to say goodbye."

Sure enough, there was Doris standing alone at the door, looking blankly in our direction. We waved, but she didn't respond. When we got back, the Captain escorted me to the front door, before going back to his post in the garden.

"There you are Soneea! I was waiting for you," said Miss Older with a big smile, holding up two cigarettes.

I shouted to Tess and Wanty Wanty that I was back and they both came out of the kitchen to hear what had happened.

"Charming!" commented Tess about the carer who'd ignored me.

"Gits!" added Wanty Wanty about everyone in the world.

"What a shame," said Miss Older, handing me her lighter "I rather liked Doris. Maybe you shouldn't answer the door anymore. It seems to bring you nothing but trouble, including me!"

She was delighted when we all laughed and after a while Louise poked her head round the door.

71

"Is the coast clear?"

It wasn't obvious what she meant at first and then she walked into the room holding her newly sterilised handbag,

"Ah good, she's gone!" she remarked. "Thank goodness. She was an odd one, that." Then she sat down in her usual chair. Miss Older shook her head and tutted,

"Who'd be old, eh?"

Chapter 23

I grabbed a quick coffee and soon enough it was time for the pre-lunch loo run. Mrs Swain had a visitor, so I decided to start with Miss Older and was hoping that Louise might be more willing to move if she had somebody else's example to follow. In the event, when I went into the lounge, I was surprised to find that Miss Older had already been to the loo and was on her way down on the chair lift. She looked really pleased with herself as she walked towards me.

"Well." I said. "I'm to be made redundant am I?"

"I'm afraid so!" she replied triumphantly. "Louise was kind enough to keep an eye on my handbag while I went upstairs and now I'm going to keep an eye on hers," she winked at me knowingly "aren't I Louise?"

"You poor darling!" announced Louise dramatically, "I don't know how you manage with your poor arm in plaster" and of her own free will, she proceeded to walk out of the lounge along the corridor towards the stairs for the very first time since we'd known her, without her precious bag! I was absolutely gobsmacked and Wanty Wanty, who'd gone outside to remind the Captain to go up soon, saw her unaccompanied and bagless sitting herself onto the chair lift and nearly fainted. He reminded her which button to press and stood watching in disbelief as she travelled to the top and completely independently walked into the bathroom and shut the door behind her.

"What have you two been up to, might I ask?" he enquired, catching sight of us standing in the lounge looking in his direction.

"It's nothing to do with me," I declared "Miss Older did it."

"You didn't hypnotize her, did you?" he questioned, pointing at her playfully.

"I shouldn't think so, dear," she laughed. "I just thought it would be helpful if I went up on my own and when I passed Louise I found myself asking her to look after my bag. It doesn't need looking after, I know that, but I was just making conversation and I thought it would help her to stop worrying about her own bag. It's nice to be useful, isn't it, dear?"

None of us was very comfortable with the way Louise had behaved over Doris. I certainly didn't feel very kindly towards her and I got the impression Miss Older didn't either, nevertheless she'd been able to put any feelings of antagonism aside and give Louise the opportunity to redeem herself, which when you think about it, was really clever. It had taken Wanty Wanty and me several months to work out how to deal with her difficult temperament, whereas Miss Older seemed to know instinctively that it was all a question of self-esteem.

In fact, when Louise came back downstairs, she had a very confident air about her and she started rifling through her bag almost at once, as if to check that it hadn't been trifled with and before lining up all her possessions on her meal trolley in the usual way, she was waylaid by the rediscovery of the paperback with no front cover. She examined it thoroughly before placing it on the meal trolley right in front of her, where it fell open about half way through at a page with the top corner folded over and extraordinarily, I say extraordinarily because we'd never seen it before, she picked it up, held it open and started reading it.

Appearances meant everything to Louise, she worked relentlessly to keep them up, which is why we grew fond of her as time went on helping us to forgive the many faux pas she made, even when it wasn't easy to.

From that day on, nearly every time she sat in the lounge, she got the same book out and went through the same routine with such confidence and flair, she gave the impression she was about to address a room full of people and deliver a lecture on Darwin's theory of evolution or something, whereas do you know what? She never actually turned the page. Not ever!

Chapter 24

After lunch, the Captain always went for a long walk and, weather permitting, Mrs Swain liked to sit in the garden in the fresh air. Everybody else preferred an afternoon nap and when I asked Miss Older what she'd like to do, she decided on the comfort of her armchair and her book. I tried to convince her of the benefits of sitting outside, because it was a lovely sunny day, but I couldn't deny it was a bit on the chilly side and didn't push it. The Captain was just leaving when I went into the lobby to get the wheelchair and Mrs Swain's coat.

"Having tea with the family. Be back late," he informed me contentedly.

"Right you are Captain, don't forget your stick."

"Never go without it," he assured me placing his cigarettes and lighter into his inside pocket. Then he put his hat on, pulled his collar up and poodled off happily down the drive.

I collected Mrs Swain and wrapped her up in her coat, hat, scarf and blanket and pushed her up the path to the back garden where we always took her, being that we could see her from the lounge window as well as from the patio doors in the apartment. The system was that she would clap her hands if she needed something and we'd soon see her.

"Now, are you sure you're warm enough, Mrs Swain. Do you need another cushion?" I asked, as I checked that the brake was firmly on.

"I'm as snug as a bug in a rug, so off you go. I'm trying to listen to the birds, if you don't mind."

"O.K. I can take a hint." I replied, feigning offence and, as I started walking back towards the front door, the fire alarm went off.

"Phew! We got out in the nick of time, didn't we?" she called out, which really tickled me in spite of my sudden panic.

"It's alright for you," I said. "I've got to go back in."

"I might as well come with you, the birds have all gone away now," she replied as I gained pace down the path.

"Tough luck!" I joked back, turning the key in the lock.

Wanty Wanty, who'd been in the kitchen setting trays with Tess when the alarm sounded, had charged along the length of the ground floor, checking for signs of smoke and shutting fire doors, and was already upstairs as far as room six when I walked in. Tess was telling Miss Older and Louise that, in the event of a fire being discovered, she would see them both out safely to the assembly point in front of the garage doors, which was precisely what we'd taught her to do, and I knew at this point that the kitchen and the apartment would have been checked first, so we were clearly in a false alarm scenario, but it was comforting to see that we were all singing from the same hymn sheet.

"Nothing up here!" shouted Wanty Wanty from upstairs, in support of my appraisal. "Turn it off would you, I'll just put the sport on for Mrs Morris."

The ear piercing shrill of the fire alarm was really loud for such a small building and was an utter nuisance to the neighbours, so we were both keen to turn it off quickly apart from which, silencing it was a sign, familiar to us all, that no fire had been discovered.

I pressed the button marked 'SILENCE ALARM' on the console and it was a relief to hear the familiar, much softer 'beep beep' sound, which in the normal way of things lasted a very short time until a green light showed indicating that the system was in 'RESET MODE'. This time, however, the beeping didn't stop and no green light appeared.

"There must be a fault." I shouted up to Wanty Wanty. Needless to say, he'd got waylaid by whatever sport he'd found on the telly and didn't hear me so I had to go up to tell him.

"Thank you Jeremy for remembering." Mrs Morris was saying. "No, not Jeremy, I mean...um... Gerald... Tsk, no, that's not right is it?" She was laughing now. "I don't know what's got into me… Jehovah, no, no, not Jehovah…" Wanty Wanty was in fits.

"There's a fault on the alarm." I said, spoiling the moment somewhat.

"Just call me Jesus, then I'll be able to perform a miracle and fix the fire alarm." suggested Wanty Wanty.

Mrs Morris didn't hear him. She was too busy wiping her eyes.

I honestly and truly only pressed the one button, but Wanty Wanty insisted I must have pressed something else. However, after consulting the instructions manual and following the procedure for resetting the alarm, he realized I was innocent of the charge, though his apology was barely audible above the persistent, now very irritating, beeping.

I went outside to tell Mrs Swain about the false alarm, leaving Wanty Wanty to call the emergency engineer, who talked him through the removal of the front cover of the apparatus and the execution of a lengthy checklist of possible easily rectifiable faults inside. The technical terminology was completely alien to Wanty Wanty, nevertheless he completed the investigation, establishing that there was indeed a fault and that an engineer would have to come out and fix it after all.

Mrs Swain informed me that soon after the alarm stopped, all the birds came back and she was happy to stay and listen to them a little longer.

Back inside, Wanty Wanty was trying to come up with a temporary solution to the constant beeping, which had started to drive him absolutely nuts.

"Do you mind if I put the radio on?" he asked Miss Older and Louise in the lounge.

Louise, who was holding her book up and looking out of the window, glared at him venomously and stopped him in his tracks.

"I don't mind," responded Miss Older "how long will it be until they fix it?"

"Anything up to 10pm, apparently."

"Can't we put some padding round it?" she proposed. "Not that it's bothering me. Being as deaf as a post does have certain advantages!"

Wanty Wanty had already opened the airing cupboard and was pulling out a duvet and a couple of pillows.

"Brilliant idea, Miss Older!" he pronounced enthusiastically and before you could say Jack Robinson he'd wrapped the duvet round the alarm console and propped the pillows on the top shelf of the corner unit immediately underneath to keep it firmly in place, instantly muffling the beeping to a friendly purr.

"There! That'll do the trick. What do you think?"

"Very professional, I must say." I replied sarcastically.

"There's never a dull moment in this place," remarked Miss Older. "Is it always as busy as this?"

"No, don't be daft." replied Wanty Wanty. "We've organized it especially for you."

"Go on with you!" she joked and we all went back to what we were doing.

Chapter 25

Mr Jones was the last of a dying breed of N.H.S. chiropodists, the only one in our area, according to the district nurse who introduced him to us. Apparently he'd been in charge of a whole team of chiropodists based at our local surgery for most of his working life. Eventually, when the facility was withdrawn, he was so close to retirement that it was decided to allow him to continue practising under the N.H.S. until he did so.

Just in case you didn't know, it was absolutely forbidden for us to cut residents' toenails, because even the tiniest lesion on the legs or feet of an elderly person has the potential to turn into an extremely serious condition. Instead, it was the duty of all rest home owners to seek the services of a qualified chiropodist and still is as far as I know.

Anyway, when Mr Jones first came to The Ivies, we thought he'd walked straight out of music hall, never mind the NHS. He had unbelievably black hair slicked down, a pencil thin moustache neatly trimmed and a silk cravat meticulously tied under the collar of an impeccably white shirt. He was quite short and slightly built, and it was a real shock when he opened his mouth and revealed a mouthful of large, impossibly white teeth.

Strangely enough, behind this façade was the most genuine person, who befriended all his customers, giving them plenty of individual attention, as if he had all the time in the world. He kept treatment notes about them all, but remembered their names and details effortlessly, in fact watching him with the residents, it seemed to me that he enjoyed his work as if it were his social life.

Mr Jones was always exactly on time and I knew that an emergency appointment on the Saturday of an Easter weekend would be no exception, which was why I made sure I got Miss Older back to her room in good time to soak her feet, not forgetting the baby oil, and dry them thoroughly before his arrival.

The first thing he invariably did, after hanging his overcoat up in the lobby, was to open the large doctor's bag he carried and take out white coat which was folded and perfectly pressed in a perspex cover, as if he'd just collected it from a professional dry cleaner and he'd shake it out and put it on. Then he'd get his notebook out, tuck his fountain pen into his top pocket and you'd know he was ready for work.

I led him towards room three and stood to one side to let him step in first and, as he approached me, I caught him glancing up at the top shelf of the corner unit, which in the normal way of things, was a fine piece of furniture, but now looked positively odd with the beeping bundle of bedding on its top shelf.

I remember the moment as one of those brief instants when not a word is spoken yet an awful lot is said. For my own part, I instinctively felt a need to explain and apologize, but couldn't do so without offending Miss Older, who was looking in our direction smiling in readiness for an introduction. For his part, the normal order of things had been put out of kilter, spoiling his entrance and making him feel uncharacteristically too shy to pass comment, but the pause was hardly noticeable and I proceeded with the introduction. Then he began to ask Miss Older the usual questions for his notes: name, date of birth, next of kin etc.

"Are you diabetic, Miss Older?" he enquired eventually.

"I shouldn't think so," she answered happily.

"And who is your GP?"

"Doctor Griffiths. Doctor J. R. Griffiths."

"Would that be the Doctor Griffiths who used to live in the big Tudor house by the green?"

"That's the one, yes."

"I'm afraid he retired years ago, I don't even think he's still alive."

"Oh dear, he can't be my doctor then. What a shame! He had a lovely wife who used to serve tea to all the patients you know."

"How charming. I'm afraid those days are well and truly gone."

Then, for some reason, they both looked up at me.

"No wonder I couldn't find him listed in the directory," I exclaimed, breaking into a grin. "We'll have to get you registered with a new doctor first thing on Tuesday. Now, would you like to join us in the lounge for tea when you've finished or shall I bring it in here?"

They both chose the lounge and just then Wanty Wanty came through the front door whistling, twittering and chirruping to Mrs Swain who was coming in for tea. She was laughing at his feeble attempt to speak to her in bird language, as he pushed her wheelchair.

"Hello Mr Jones!" he called out brightly. "What do you think of our new fire detection equipment? Miss Older designed it you know." He had a real knack with people and always made them feel comfortable.

"Most inventive!" replied Mr Jones, entering into the spirit of things. "I must review the questionnaire for my customers and add 'Hidden talents' to the list, you never know when I might need one of them."

Then he complemented Miss Older, much to her amusement, on her clever innovation.

Chapter 26

Every Saturday, Bessie's son and daughter-in -law used to bring a fish and chip supper for the three of them to eat together straight off the paper. It was a ritual they'd started fifty years previously when they got married and had stuck to religiously ever since.

If you remember, Bessie was the lady in room five who hated foreign food (and blue water) and was 101 years old when we first took over. It was the strangest thing in the world to see a man struggle up the stairs to visit his mother, looking more like a resident than her.

His wife was actually fairly mobile, but he'd been born with a fault in one of his hips, which had led to the shortening of one of his legs. He'd had a pronounced limp throughout his life and eventually developed arthritis, which reduced his mobility and caused him to gain a great deal of weight. It was because of his weight that he had to struggle up the stairs instead of using the chair lift.

On that particular Saturday, when Wanty Wanty opened the door to them both, the engineer, who thankfully had come to fix the fire alarm sooner rather than later, was standing on his step ladder dismantling the apparatus and Mr Jones, the chiropodist, who'd had a second cup of tea and stayed to chat longer than he intended, was just about to leave.

The hallway was like Piccadilly Circus when I looked along from the lounge, before starting the pre-supper loo run.

Tess was taking a cup of tea to the engineer, whose tool bag was at the bottom of his ladder right in the gangway and Mr Jones was using up the width of the hallway with his doctor's bag, which left very little room for Bessie's outsized son and wife to manoeuvre past with their parcels of fish and chips. Wanty Wanty was pressing himself back against the door of room three in an attempt to make more space. He would have been able to get himself out of the way altogether by standing in the doorway, in the normal way of things, but all the doors in the house were shut for the benefit of the fire engineer.

There was nothing I could do except wait. It was all very bad timing because Mrs Swain, Miss Older and especially Louise would need to go to the loo any time soon.

"Would you like me to move my bag out of the way?" suggested the engineer, not unreasonably.

"No, it's alright," replied Wanty Wanty, *utterly* unreasonably and then commanded in sudden traffic warden mode, "Outward bound to the left, inward to the right please." In truth, the engineer should have put his bag in the recess under his ladder in the first place, for safety reasons, if nothing else and, if I'd have let him in, that's what I'd have asked him to do. Wanty Wanty didn't like telling people what to do though, so the engineer had taken full advantage of his good nature and made himself at home.

Anyway, Mr Jones then found it necessary to exchange pleasantries with the engineer as well as Bessie's relatives, making it look like he was never going to leave, so Wanty Wanty went to fetch his coat and held it open, hoping to spur him in the direction of the front door, but blow me down, Bessie's son began a debate with the engineer about quantum mechanics, or something, which stopped anybody from moving and trapped his wife between the tool bag at the bottom of the ladder and Mr Jones' doctor's bag, not only that, but Tess was cornered as well. There was no way she was going to get past, so she disappeared into room three to make an early start on turning the beds down.

"If you start pushing me along the hall, they'll move out of the way," whispered Mrs Swain "wheelchairs always have that effect on people!"

"Good thinking. What would I do without you?" I replied, putting the plan into action and as soon as we passed Louise's room, Bessie's son moved towards the staircase, so his wife could step round the tool bag and Mr Jones could head for the front door, then he wound up the debate.

"It's probably nothing more than a fuse," he stated, partly jokingly and partly in a deliberate attempt to undermine the engineer. Then he turned towards the stairs.

Tess came out of room three in time to catch this and we had to avoid eye contact to stop ourselves from laughing - there was no Wanty Wanty to help us out this time.

Bessie's son placed the fish and chips on the chair lift and heaved himself slowly up the stairs, one at a time holding onto the banister and his wife followed. This left me enough room to turn the wheelchair to face the chair lift and Tess enough room to get passed. Rather than stand there doing nothing while they made their way up, I moved the tool bag out of the way, then I picked up the three parcels of fish and chips and followed them up. I knew that, if I didn't, they'd do what they usually did, which was to call the chair lift up as if it were a dumb waiter, and we'd have had to wait an awful long time for the damn thing to come back down again. Before handing over their supper, I offered to plate the individual meals and heat them up. Luckily, their expressions told me immediately this was utter heresy.

Meanwhile downstairs, Wanty Wanty had helped Mrs Swain on to the chair lift, having evidently said a final goodbye to Mr Jones, and was on his way up with her.

"Can we move along please? Do we have to cause a traffic jam at the top of the stairs as well as at the bottom?" he called up, still in traffic warden mode.

"I wouldn't upset him if I were you," improvised Mrs Swain.

"Awfully sorry officer!" volunteered the wife "the old man is having trouble with his gear stick."

There was no way of telling if she realised what she'd said and I looked at Wanty Wanty biting my lip helplessly. Before he had a chance to come to the rescue however, Mrs Swain said, with a completely straight face and quite obviously to the wife,

"Oh, you poor thing!" and brought the house down.

On hearing the commotion, Bessie came out of her room, which made us all stop laughing, like naughty children.

"Got your fish and chips, mum, and your pea fritter," they informed her and they all went in to have their supper.

Wanty Wanty went to see to Edith and Mrs Morris, as usual, and I helped Mrs Swain before checking in on Florence.

When I took Mrs Swain back down, she asked if she could have supper in the lounge, which wasn't unusual at the weekend or any time sandwiches were on the menu.

" It's the only meal I can get into my mouth without throwing all over the shop." she'd say.

"It's your turn to go up first, dear," Miss Older was shouting to Louise.

"I'll look after your bag again."

"Thank you darling. You poor thing, I don't know how you manage with that arm in plaster."

She closed her book and placed it on her meal trolley, which she pushed to one side and then she made her way to the stairs. I got Mrs Swain a meal trolley and positioned it under her feet while she stayed in the wheelchair. She didn't like all the palaver of having to move onto an armchair and then back onto the wheelchair again after eating, then I glanced at Miss Older, who was following Louise with her eyes and when she heard the chair lift starting up, she beamed a satisfied smile at me.

"Not just a one off then" I said.

"Are you still there, Miss Older?" enquired Mrs Swain.

"Yes, it's me dear" she replied and then she bellowed out the whole story about Louise, the loo phobia and the handbag, which of course was actually meant to be a confidence, but the engineer couldn't help overhearing the whole thing.

I went upstairs to see if Louise had actually gone into the bathroom and found that instead she'd walked straight past it and up the three steps to the top landing.

"Ah, there you are Louise!" Wanty Wanty exclaimed, emerging just then from room six "And what can I do for Madame on this splendid Saturday evening?"

"Have you seen a black handbag?"

"That'll be the one Miss Older's keeping an eye on downstairs, I think you'll find."

"Thank you. Which way is that?"

"Follow me, Madame, I'll show you" and he led the way to the top of the stairs where I was standing.

"You were on your way to the loo," I reminded her in as friendly a way as possible, whilst denying her access to the chair lift.

"I'll get my bag first, if you don't mind" she retorted in her familiar defiant way.

Surely she couldn't have been to the loo in such a short space of time, we were both thinking, and we both knew that if she went downstairs to get her bag, it was going to be the devil's own job to get her to go back up again. We looked at each other silently. This newfound independence was proving to be troublesome. The fact that the bathroom door was open was a dead giveaway though, because, if you remember, we always kept it open as a sign that it was free. It was a system the other residents were familiar with, whereas Louise wasn't able to retain the information and always made a point of closing the door when she came out.

"Aha!" exclaimed Wanty Wanty unexpectedly, "Here it is!" and he walked or more accurately, pranced, into the bathroom.

"Where?" asked Louise, following him in.

"Here!" he replied, pointing at the toilet.

She looked momentarily bemused. So did I to be honest.

"Here's the loo!" he continued. "I'll just get your bag." He came out and closed the door. "I'll be outside waiting for you."

"Thank you, I shan't be long," she mumbled.

It was a complete confidence trick, but it was brilliant, because it worked.

"I'll see if Tess needs any help" I informed Wanty Wanty, as I walked downstairs.

"Blimey, it's like Faulty Towers in here!" remarked the engineer, when I passed his ladder. "How do you stay sane?"

It was meant in a friendly, complimentary way, I'm sure, but I didn't like it. He'd been in the home for well over an hour, which was already an intrusion. Making crass comments was stepping over the line in my book. What upset me in particular, was the fact that he'd witnessed Wanty Wanty and me patronizing Louise. To be honest, patronizing a person only qualified as patronizing when the person was aware of it, which Louise clearly wasn't, but he wouldn't have necessarily known that and the fact that an outsider had been privy to the event made me feel that we hadn't respected her dignity somehow. Do you know what I mean?

"Actually, there isn't a sane person in this house." I found myself saying, without stopping or looking up at him. " If I were you, I'd make sure I got the job finished and got out of here before dark."

On reflection, it was ruder than necessary, which was confirmed by his short burst of uncomfortable laughter, but I simply didn't have the same high tolerance levels as Wanty Wanty.

Tess had finished turning the beds down as well as delivering the tablets and night time drinks to the ground floor rooms and I went to find her in the kitchen, where Wanty Wanty presently joined us, because it was fast approaching supper time. I had difficulty telling them about the incident with the engineer above the noise of the fire alarm, which he continued to test more times than I thought absolutely necessary, but they both agreed it wasn't really his place to pass comment and finally he knocked on the door to announce that the fault had been rectified and he handed Wanty Wanty the documentation for signing.

"What was the problem exactly?" enquired Wanty Wanty. The engineer looked at Tess and me with a knowing smile and I warmed to him, as he answered the question.

"Just a fuse" he chuckled and, as soon as we brought Wanty Wanty up to speed, we all absolutely cracked up.

Chapter 27

The Captain came home at about six thirty. I heard the front door slam shut when I was with Mrs Swain in room three. Wanty Wanty was in room six immediately above and he too would have heard the door closing.

I helped Mrs Swain out of her wheelchair and back into her armchair and watched the Captain walk towards the lounge where Miss Older was waiting for me to join her, cigarettes and lighter at the ready.

"Ah, another smoker. How nice!" I heard him comment, as I followed him into the room.

"Would you like one?" enquired Miss Older, holding out her packet of Benson and Hedges.

"Bit strong for me thanks. Better stick to these mild ones" he replied politely and he took his Silk Cut out of his pocket and put them on the table with his lighter.

"Hello Captain!" I interrupted "The boss was looking for you upstairs."

This wasn't strictly true of course. I just knew that Wanty Wanty would be on the alert to get him to the loo.

"Yes, wanted a word with him too, actually" and he went off to find him.

"Shall we wait for him, dear?" shouted Miss Older at the top of her voice at the same time as the phone rang in the kitchen.

"Yes, let's. I'll just answer that." I said opening the door. She looked at me blankly and I knew she hadn't heard the phone or me for that matter, so I picked up the receiver and walked back into the lounge with it pressed to my ear.

"Hello, The Ivies, Sonia speaking." I answered in my telephone voice.

She evidently hadn't seen a cordless phone before, because her blankness intensified.

"It's the Captain's daughter," I explained holding my hand over the mouthpiece.

"I see dear," she clearly hadn't, if her expression was anything to go by.

"I'm ringing to make sure daddy got back alright," said the Captain's daughter and without waiting for a reply, " he hasn't had his beer yet. I didn't give him one. I thought he'd have something to look forward to that way."

"That's a relief, the boss felt quite deprived earlier. He'll be dead pleased when I tell him."

Meanwhile, the Captain was upstairs telling Wanty Wanty he hadn't had a beer yet, because his daughter had taken him to a fund raising buffet at the Vicarage, where the choice of drinks was limited to tea or lemonade. Wanty Wanty couldn't be sure he wasn't making the whole thing up, but he promised to get

them both a beer in any case, just as soon as he'd been to the loo (the Captain that is).

Miss Older was fascinated by the cordless phone and truly amazed that you could walk through the whole house with it as well as take it round the garden. To be honest most of the residents together with many relatives were fascinated by it too, as many people still didn't have the facility. In general, rest homes had payphones for outgoing calls only, or individual phones in residents' rooms, which had to be paid for in addition to the fee. A telephone that could be taken to any resident in the home was quite a rarity. Imagine what they'd make of our mobile phones today!

Having said that, people over seventy didn't usually get on very well with phones of any kind in those days. You had the type who'd never speak on the phone at any cost; then you had the type who'd point and gesticulate as if the person on the other end of the line could see; the type who held the receiver upside down and upon not hearing anything, knocked it repeatedly on the arm of the chair or into the palm of their hand until it came apart at the seams and finally the type who'd start shouting or keep saying "Hello, hello, can you hear me? Are you still there?" for absolutely no reason whatsoever.

Anyhow, Miss Older handed me a cigarette and soon enough the Captain came to join us, whereupon I told him about his daughter's call which legitimised Wanty Wanty's sudden disappearance into the kitchen to get the promised beers. Then we all sat down together for an impromptu social gathering, or more accurately, all of us except the Captain sat down.

He stood by the table most of the time, flicking his ash into the ashtray over and over again, swaying from side to side with his beer in his hand. Occasionally he sat for a second, got up again, took a few steps forward, then back and in between times he rearranged his cigarettes and lighter, standing the packet up, then laying it down, placing the lighter on top and then lining it up by its side.

"How you haven't spilled all your beer or set light to yourself is a complete mystery" remarked Wanty Wanty.

"Mm" voiced the Captain, checking the contents of his glass.

"Isn't this nice?" bellowed Miss Older.

It *was* nice and we agreed with her wholeheartedly.

By the time we finished telling the Captain about the hectic afternoon he'd missed and had the last puffs of our cigarettes, Miss Older was exhausted. She said good night to the Captain and made her way towards her room.

I followed her along the hall and was pleased to see she was taking more confident steps, putting her full weight down and peeling her feet off properly, but you could tell she was tired because, when she started to talk, she had to stand still.

"I've had more things happen to me in these two days than I've had happen to me in ten years" she puffed. "I don't know what I'll do with myself all day when I go home."

"Let's cross that bridge when we get to it, shall we?" I suggested.

"Did you mean to say *we*, Soneea?"

"Well I'm not going to abandon you, now am I?"

"You were quite happy to abandon *me*, in favour of your new smokers' circle!" piped up Mrs Swain from room three, which we were fast approaching.

"We have an open door policy for new members" I shouted, so Miss Older could hear, "don't we Miss Older?"

"New members of what?"

"The smokers' circle."

"Ooh yes we do, don't we dear?" she grinned.

"Look," said Mrs Swain "as much as I hate to disappoint you, I'm not in the slightest bit interested. I'd only end up throwing ash all over the place and burn holes in everything, that's assuming I put the right end in my mouth!"

We all laughed at this unlikely image and, while I was drawing the privacy curtain across the room, Miss Older, who was standing right in front of Mrs Swain by then, leaned in towards her and pretended to whisper,

"Perhaps it's for the best dear, we don't want to set the fire alarms off again, do we?" and she went to sit on her bed as if she'd been familiar with the routine for ages.

If only I'd closed the door first instead of drawing the curtains, Bessie's son wouldn't have seen me, but he was on his way down the stairs just as I went to close it.

"The Mrs wants a word with you, if you've got a minute." he said. "I'll be waiting in the car."

Damn! I was hoping to avoid his wife in particular. She always wanted 'a word' when she visited. The following Saturday was going to be her mother-in-law's birthday and I knew she'd be wanting to tell me (for the umpteenth time) what the arrangements were, falling as she did into the category of over seventy year olds who never spoke on the phone at any cost, so I just about had enough time to get Mrs Swain over to her bed, organize the trolleys with bowls of hot water and toiletries for them both, before I heard her coming down the stairs.

I held the lobby door open for her and followed her out while she told me what she told me the previous Saturday and the Saturday before that: they wouldn't be bringing fish and chips for supper they'd be coming at 3.30 instead, just in time for tea, she'd be making the cake, big enough to go round, nice sponge, they'd bring three candles, not a *hundred* and three, (the cake wasn't *that* big, ha, ha!) no fuss, Mum didn't like fuss and, oh, could I make sure she wore her new dress and cardigan.

I tried to look as if I was hearing it all for the first time and even laughed in the right place, but I opened the front door while she was still talking, just in case she decided to repeat it all over again, I really didn't think I could take it all over again without screaming.

I went back to room three and while I finished getting Mrs Swain and Miss Older ready for bed, I told them about Bessie reaching the grand old age of a hundred and three.

"I sincerely hope I don't live that long," stated Mrs Swain "promise you'll bump me off before then."

"Only if you lie down and go to sleep." I joked back while I tucked her in.

When I went round to Miss Older, who was already lying down, she was taking her watch off and putting it with the other things on her bedside table.

"There we are dear," she tried really hard to whisper, "torch, tissues and wristwatch all ready for use" and then she reached out for my hand and held it tight.

"I wouldn't mind how long I lived," she added, "as long as I was here with you Soneea."

"You'll be sick to death of me in no time at all." I assured her, trying to lighten things up a bit.

"Never!" she replied smiling and as she let go of my hand, her eyes were already closing.

Chapter 28

Miss Older's very spontaneous display of affection and trust after just a couple of days was something we'd seen in the Captain, Mrs W and Mrs Swain, who were the three residents admitted to the home after we'd taken over and we'd settled into the job. Just like her, they were all friendly and trusting from the outset, holding us instinctively in high regard.

The Captain for example had seen Wanty Wanty in the post office many a time before the 'Skipper' incident and had often exchanged the odd pleasantry with him, so when he moved in, he found a familiar face and in any case, had heard good reports from the local people we'd got to know.

Then Mrs W grew fond of us as a result of witnessing all the hard work we put into caring for her very frail husband, who'd moved into room three with her. When he died, she was already settled into the routine, surrounded by people she knew she could trust and she was able to grieve without feeling too lonely.

Finally Mrs Swain clicked with me instantly when I went to assess her in the geriatric hospital, where she'd been for months, and hers is a story I simply must tell you in a little more detail.

Given the fact that she was blind and chair bound, I told the social worker in charge of her case, I couldn't bear the thought of her knowing that the purpose of my visit was an assessment, just in case I'd have to turn her down. The social worker suggested she tell her I was a colleague who needed to meet her for a second opinion regarding her needs and I agreed to go along with it because she was desperate to find a placement. None of the rest homes would accept a blind person, none of the homes for the blind would accept an elderly person and it was beginning to look like nursing care was going to be her only option, which was so unfair, because nursing homes charged a hell of a lot more than residential care homes and, she didn't need actual nursing care.

When I found Mrs Swain in the local hospital in a wheelchair among at least fifty others, lined up in what was supposed to be the 'Day Room', but could at best only be described as a corridor, I introduced myself simply as Sonia and let her speak first.

"I hope to God you've come to get me out of here." she said as she shook my hand. Then she placed her other hand on top gazing into nothingness. "Your hands don't feel like social workers' hands, they feel like the hands of somebody who has to work for a living!"

"Shush!" I warned her in jest, instantly impressed with her lovely personality "You never know who might be listening" and, feeling obliged to come clean, I told her what I'd said to her social worker.

"Why on earth would you have to turn me down?" she asked. "I'd be the perfect asset. You'll have to make your mind up quickly though, everyone's fighting over me now."

"I can well believe it." I said. "Can you stand up and walk if somebody helps you?"

"Only when I'm sober," she replied straight-faced.

"In that case, you're in." I told her and, if there hadn't been a procedure to follow, she would have left with me there and then, what's more, I would have taken her.

The five residents already living in the rest home when we took over, on the other hand, were a completely different kettle of fish. They appeared standoffish, suspicious and very guarded - although in reality they were more bewildered than anything else - and when you hear what happened on our first day, you'll understand better why that was, as well as why it took a lot of patience and a lot of hard work over a lot longer than a couple of days to win *their* confidence.

When we drove towards the property at 9am as arranged, absolutely thrilled and excited to have completed the purchase in spite of the many tedious setbacks I won't bore you with, there was a car outside on the street, which sped away rather suspiciously, we thought. Then we found the front door wide open and, in the lobby on the windowsill a grubby old folder marked RESIDENTS with two sets of keys on top. We rang the doorbell and looked inside the folder, where we found five sheets of foolscap paper, one for each resident, with their respective room numbers and only their basic details. There was no forwarding address or phone number. Meanwhile nobody answered the door and we let ourselves in knowing that something very fishy was going on.

Soon enough we discovered that absolutely nothing in the way of the very bare essentials to run a rest home, let alone any of the items listed in the inventory had been left on the premises.

There was no furniture whatsoever in the residents lounge, no curtains or light bulbs either. In the kitchen there were no appliances, no table, no crockery, cutlery or trays, no instructions for the central heating and hot water system, no drugs lists, notes or care plans. There was no linen in the airing cupboard and not even a loo roll in the residents' toilets!

"I've never been sure about this minimalist look" stated Wanty Wanty, ever the comedian, "Let's go and see if they've left us any residents!"

We walked round the home with the sadly inadequate pieces of foolscap paper as our guide.

ROOM ONE, MRS LOUISE STOCKWELL

Wanty Wanty knocked a deliberate confident sort of knock. After a long wait Louise opened the door just a smidgen and peered through the gap.

"I'm rather busy at the minute, if you don't mind." she said sharply and she shut the door without waiting for us to speak. Rooms two and three were vacant, so we moved on.

ROOM FOUR, MISS FLORENCE PROCTER.

Wanty Wanty knocked a less deliberate, less confident sort of knock. "Just a minute...ooh jibber this wretched leg...oh lordy be with you in a tic... nearly there now, here I am..." came Florence's voice from within and after a lot of banging and crashing she opened the door and wedged herself between it and the doorframe.

"Hello," I said. "We've come to introduce ourselves, we're the new owners. I'm Sonia and this…."

"Pleased to meet you I'm sure" she interrupted, avoiding eye contact. "Nobody said anything to me about new owners…don't you be worrying yourselves about me…I don't need much…I've always looked after myself…my folk'll tell you…they come every Wednesday they get me everything I need…jibber, this leg's punishment…ooh jibber, can't stand for long, must get on…" and she struggled away from the self closing door and let it shut behind her.

ROOM FIVE, MRS BESSIE JOHNS.

Wanty Wanty knocked a decidedly feeble sort of knock.

"Come on in." called out Bessie shuffling her newspaper. I did the introduction.

"Nobody tells me nothing round here" she stated nonchalantly, whilst turning the page. "It don't make no difference to me, I don't care who runs the place."

ROOM SIX.

A) MISS EDITH CAMPBELL.

B) MRS NORMA MORRIS.

Wanty Wanty made *me* knock on this, the last door. No reply was the answer, so we opened it and peered gingerly round. Edith looked at us and frowned. Mrs Morris was slumped asleep in her armchair.

"'Scuse me, can we come in?" I enquired.

"LEAVE MY MONEY ALONE YOU THIEVING BUGGERS YOU!" hollered Edith, suddenly and loudly enough to waken the dead.

Mrs Morris stirred a little then slumped back again.

"Brilliant. Great start!" complained Wanty Wanty sarcastically, as we made our way back down the stairs.

In all honesty, none of it came as much of a surprise. We'd seen how neglected the residents all were, as well as how run down the whole place was on our first viewing, in addition to which, we'd come to hate the previous owners with a passion during the months of negotiation when they'd been unpleasant, unreliable, dishonest and extremely trying, so there was no telling what they'd do to make the handover as difficult as they possibly could. Mind you, we didn't think for a minute they'd neglect to prepare the residents for our arrival and certainly didn't expect them to remove the entire contents, especially as they were so shabby. Doing a runner and deliberately landing us in the proverbial was the last straw, so as punishment, we nicknamed them Spit and Gob. That would teach them!

Seriously though, it was a nasty blow, as the original plan had been to make use of the sub-standard items listed in the inventory until we refurbished one room at a time. In the event we were obliged to act with rather more urgency and quickly make a list of some basic essentials, which Wanty Wanty went off to buy, while I got on the phone to contact Mr Halliday, who was the social worker in charge of our registration application. He'd proven to be surprisingly supportive during the whole process, keeping in regular contact through the long sales transaction afterwards and we thought he might be able to help. In any case, he needed to know the predicament the residents had been left in.

One stroke of good fortune was the fact that telephones remained the property of the G.P.O. (General Post Office) in those days, whatever the circumstances. They were only ever rented to the customer and couldn't be unplugged or moved around as they can today. Had this not been the case, Spit and Gob would most certainly have taken the phone along with everything else, effectively cutting us off from the outside world.

In the event, I got through to Mr Halliday and relayed the news to him. He didn't seem in the least bit surprised, in fact it was as if he'd been expecting the call.

"I'll be there as soon as I can" was all he said.

I replaced the receiver (which is what you did with a phone when you finished your call) and I walked round the shabby kitchen trying to visualize what changes we might make and wishing to God I'd brought some cleaning equipment instead of packing it all up for the removal men, who wouldn't be

97

arriving until late afternoon. Naively, we'd imagined we'd get stuck into whatever instructions Spit and Gob would leave after they finished the early morning shift and there'd be no point in getting our belongings until later in the day, but they'd literally walked off with everything. There was nothing to make mid morning coffees or lunch with and I couldn't even find a broom to sweep the flipping floor with.

I walked through to the owners' accommodation and when I saw the state it had been left in, I was overcome by a sudden homesickness and an overwhelming urge to cry my bloody eyes out. Just then though, I caught sight of Wanty Wanty struggling up the footpath towards the extension overloaded with carrier bags and this brought a smile to my face, spurring me in the direction of our private front door, which I opened in a proud 'new lady of the house' sort of way.

As I helped Wanty Wanty with his load, he told me how inventive he'd been, turning his trip to the local shops into a public relations exercise. He'd introduced himself to the shopkeepers and told them all about Spit and Gob, the terrible state of the home and the residents, what we planned to do to put it right and promised them invitations to our intended open day. On top of all that, he'd bought everything on the list, including a set of cups and saucers from the charity shop, he'd ordered fish and chips for everybody's lunch, to be collected at 12.30 and more brilliantly, he'd picked up a ready chilled bottle of bubbly, which we were just about to have a glass of (I mean cup of) when the doorbell rang. It was Mr Halliday, who'd already turned up with a large van. One of us would need to go with him, he explained, so as to choose whatever urgent items were needed from a storage place belonging to the council. We could have them on loan and return them in due course. Wanty Wanty had done so well with the shopping, I was sure he could also be trusted with this task and I was happy to go off and get 'half tenses' organized for the residents.

I unloaded the shopping and washed up the charity tea set, then I prized the new kettle out of its box, put it on and looked round for something I might use as a tray. There wasn't anything remotely resembling a tray and, after unsuccessfully trying to remove a small shelf from one of the kitchen units, I went off to check the two vacant rooms.

In room two there was nothing but a pile of rubbish and in room three there was a nasty looking commode, a large cardboard box spilling over with porn magazines of all things and a rickety old bedside table. This last item was of the type with a small drawer and a locker beneath and the top of it was badly stained with old rings of tea or coffee. I dragged it into the hall, put it next to an electric point and covered it with my headscarf. Then I pulled the drawer right out to use as a tray and made a functional, if somewhat basic servery. As I didn't know how each resident liked their coffee, I thought it would be more efficient to get the kettle and things from the kitchen and make the drinks to order, one resident at a time, serving the sugar, milk and biscuits straight from the containers, there in the hall where nobody could see.

I went to each room, tapped lightly on the door, opened it ever so slightly without waiting for a reply and called out in a familiar sort of way,

"Do you want sugar in your coffee, darling?" then " How much milk?" and finally "Biscuits?"

Not exactly the standard I'd gone on about to the famous fat face, when trying to get a business loan, more like a transport caff to tell the truth, nevertheless it did the trick and when I served Louise, Florence and Bessie, they seemed a little friendlier as they each handed me a dirty mug left on their meal trolleys since breakfast. I could hardly believe my eyes, when I saw them. They were the kind of mugs you might find on a building site. You know, all stained and chipped, haphazardly brought along without any attempt to match them up and in any case, far too heavy for frail fingers. One was a commemorative mug from Lady Diana and Prince Charles' wedding, one had pictures of naked women in provocative poses all over it and another was covered in views of

Blackpool pier. Even the tattiest transport caff could do better than that.

Not expecting any response from Edith and Mrs Morris in room six, I took the milk and sugar in with their coffees. Mrs Morris was still slumped in her chair, so I saw to Edith first, apologizing for the lack of decorum as I spooned the sugar out of the packet.

"Is one enough?" I enquired.

She lowered her head, put her hand just above her eyebrows, as if about to salute and pressed her temple with the thumb of the same hand in what would eventually become a familiar gesture.

"You have it, dear. You look as if you need it more than me" she retorted unreasonably.

"I've had mine, thank you. This one's for you and look there's a nice chocolate biscuit as well. O.K?"

She peeped through two of her fingers and when I moved out of sight, she reached for the biscuit and dunked it into her coffee.

It took ages to wake Mrs Morris up and when I eventually succeeded I realized she was a stroke victim, because she began to lean too dangerously to the left to drink her coffee, so I took the pillows from her bed and arranged them between her shoulder and the wing of the chair to prop her up in the hope that she'd be able to manage without too much help.

Meanwhile, having ruffled the bed, I thought I'd better tidy it up and, on smoothing down the top sheet, I noticed how flimsy the mattress was. It was a good job I didn't lean on it actually, because I'd have fallen flat on my face if I had, since hidden under the faded threadbare counterpane, it turned out to be a great deal wider than its metal base, overlapping by a good six inches or more on both sides. Slightly troubled by the discovery, I decided to inspect both beds and stripped them off. It was just as well I did. There were no bottom sheets, just filthy pieces of tatty waterproof material of some kind at the top ends and the bottom ends were absolutely soaking wet. Edith's even had a puddle on the floor underneath.

When Wanty Wanty and Mr Halliday returned with the vanload of equipment and more shopping from a nearby supermarket, I told them about the condition of the two beds and they quite literally did a u-turn to go back and collect the six nearly new beds they'd left behind, on the assumption we didn't need them.

During this second journey, Mr Halliday told Wanty Wanty that, had we not decided to buy 'Ivy's Rest Home', the authorities would have closed it down. He said he would probably have lost his job, had he given us this information before we exchanged contracts. He'd desperately wanted to, so as to give us more clout to push everybody into action and speed up the sale, not least because he'd had many a sleepless night fretting about the residents being left with Spit and Gob, who were seriously dodgy. He'd been counting the days for us to take over and had borrowed a van in anticipation of our call. Well I never!

Mr Halliday spent the rest of the day with us, lugging the new beds and the furniture into the home and loading up the van with the old beds and all the rubbish, including the porn magazines, for the tip. We had no idea what on earth we'd have done without him and do you know what? We never, ever saw him again. Can you believe it? When we phoned his office to speak to him about returning all the stuff, we were told he no longer worked for the department and his whereabouts were unknown. Wanty Wanty was convinced he must have lost his job after all,

"He used his own initiative. They don't like that sort of thing in government departments" he pronounced, getting on his soapbox, "Do what you're told to do, ask permission before you do anything you haven't been told to do and fill the forms in. That's what they like."

If you're out there Mr Halliday, we so badly wanted you to see how we transformed the home, how seriously we took our job and how right you were to believe in us. We've never forgotten you or what you did for us.

Chapter 29

I know I've digressed again, but don't worry I haven't lost the thread. If you recall, I'd got to the Saturday evening, when Miss Older was falling asleep as she let go of my hand.

As I shut the bedroom door and walked towards the kitchen, active duty completed, I felt as if she'd been with us for much longer than two days and I was really happy with the progress she'd made in that short time, especially as her arrival had been unexpected.

Tess had a gig that evening at her school 'Teen Club' (T C's for short) and she was already waiting for me to take her there, the transition from domestic assistant to rock chick, effortlessly achieved.

While I was gone, Wanty Wanty put the dinner on and then he poured the drinks in preparation for the mutual admiration society meeting. Both went down very smoothly indeed, especially as we had so much to talk about, what with Louise's bag, the fire alarm and the gaffe about the gear stick, enough material to keep potential visitors entertained for a long time to come. Then we came up with a possible solution to Miss Older's predicament.

It was imperative to have some sort of plan, as Mrs W would be back on Friday afternoon, which was approaching faster than you might think, considering Monday was a bank holiday, Tuesday Wanty Wanty's day off and Wednesday mine. Day care, that's what we'd offer. It wouldn't be too difficult for

one of us to collect her at 7am before early morning tea and take her home at 7pm after the residents were done. She was used to being on her own and didn't need help during the night, so it would be the perfect set up for her. We'd need to contact her solicitor, who was named as acting next of kin, and we'd need to get a social worker on board as well as her doctor, once we'd got her registered with one. She could presumably go back home full time after her plaster was removed in about six weeks. We decided it was best not to mention the idea to her until we'd liased with the various parties and worked out what to charge. She was obviously happy with us and it would have been insensitive to risk building her hopes up, just in case she couldn't afford it or there were any objections.

Before too long it was time to collect Tess, who'd made such an impression with the audience that she'd secured herself a regular spot at T.C's. All three of us went to bed feeling much like Miss Older, absolutely exhausted, but content.

Chapter 30

It truly felt as if I'd only just dropped off, but it was already five o'clock in the morning when this almighty crash from the direction of Florence's room above the kitchen woke me up with a start.

As was the norm when anything went bump in the night, Wanty Wanty was instantaneously and inexplicably propelled out of bed straight into his clothes. On this occasion, he was already half way up the stairs when I came to and at Florence's door by the time I reached the staircase still half asleep.

"Ooh jibber jibber...silly, silly me...oh dear, oh dear, come in...please come in." I could hear Florence whimpering, as I made my way up.

Wanty Wanty meanwhile appeared to be struggling with the door, which would only open a few inches.

"Thank the Lord you're here...ooh jibber...what a big silly...come in, come in... please help me..."

"If I could only open the door Florence my dear" he began, in a desperate attempt not to sound impatient "I'd already be in there helping you, now wouldn't I? How many times have we told you how dangerous it is to barricade yourself in, hmm?"

It was something she'd got into the habit of doing when Spit and Gob still ran the home, because she'd apparently never felt safe, especially at night.

"They weren't like you the other lot...oh no, not like you" she told us once she learned to trust us. "Hardly ever saw *her* mind...it was him who ran the place...if you can call it 'running'...proper little Hitler he was...stomping around...shouting...I wouldn't trust him as far as I could throw him, never did trust him, you can't trust somebody who serves your morning tea wearing nothing but his underpants...honest to goodness, nothing but his underpants!" All the residents confirmed this story, as they did the many other extraordinary things she told us, so it was hardly surprising she'd become reclusive. In the end however, after a lot of TLC, a few outings downstairs to meet other residents and repeated reassurances about the lock-up procedure, she did actually stop barricading herself in, which is why we were both disappointed and surprised that she was regressing to her old habit for no apparent reason, especially when it became clear that it was her bloody commode pressed up against the door.

"I daren't use any sudden force," explained Wanty Wanty "it might fall over."

The prospect of the contents of a commode spilling over wasn't a pleasant one under any circumstances, but the brand new carpet was at stake and the look of horror on my face gave him renewed determination to stretch his arm through the gap and round the door, press his chest and cheek up against it with all his might and ever so gradually lift the damn thing ever so slightly out of the way. I was a lot thinner in those days and was able to squeeze through the small gap he managed to make, then move the offending item and eventually open the door. At that precise moment, our cat Percy unexpectedly flew out from under the bed and shot past us like a bat out of hell, letting out a blood-curdling wail as it careered uncontrollably down the stairs.

I should tell you at this juncture that Florence adored Percy and used to regularly coax him up to her window from the flat roof of the extension with cat treats her relatives used to buy for her. Strictly speaking, he wasn't allowed in the residents' bedrooms, a rule he usually respected without fail, but he couldn't resist the cat treats and we turned a blind eye because it gave Florence so much pleasure and her room was coincidentally the only one overlooking the flat roof. We did make it clear that she should put him out at night though and, as far as we knew, she did.

Anyway, Florence was on the floor under the window, fully dressed and wedged in by her armchair, which usually lived opposite her bed on the other side of the room. In some confusion all around her were two cushions, her pillows, several scattered clothes pegs and her brown leather pouffe. We moved it all out of the way to reach her and assess the damage.

"A little help to get me up…that's all I need…bless you…thank you for coming… lordy lordy, what a muddle…"

She hadn't broken anything, but she was very distressed and there was a nasty skin flap on her arm. While checking for other injuries, we manoeuvred her into the sitting position then Wanty Wanty stood behind her and bent down hooking both his arms under hers. I grabbed hold of her from under her knees and we heaved her onto the armchair and propped her dodgy leg up on the pouffe, which is what it was actually for, all the while attempting to soothe her spirit with kind words of reassurance.

"I'll get you a nice early cup of tea," promised Wanty Wanty for example "you'll be as right as rain in no time."
He fetched the first aid kit from the sideboard on the landing before going off to put the kettle on, leaving me to smooth Florence's skin back, look for any other cuts or bruises and listen to what she had to say.

Interspersed with her usual 'jibbers', she told me that she'd forgotten all about Percy and, before getting ready for bed, she'd put the pouffe on top of the seat of the armchair and lugged it over to the window to use as a ladder for the purpose of pegging her curtains together. Yep, that's right, pegging her curtains together. She'd then wedged the pillows and cushions around the pouffe to stop it from wobbling and she'd climbed on to it, so as to reach right up to the top of the curtain and ensure that there'd be absolutely no gaps. Afterwards, she'd put everything back and had sat down for a minute to get her breath back, but had fallen asleep and the next thing she'd known, the cat was meowing to go out, so she'd gone through the same rigmarole to let it out of the window and in her haste had inevitably lost her balance, crashed to the floor and frightened the poor creature half to death, hence its sudden appearance from its hiding place under the bed.

Florence was a fiercely independent and very private person, who found it excruciatingly painful to need help of any kind. As far as she was concerned, needing help was a definite sign of vulnerability, which not only allowed people to take advantage, but made her feel insecure as well. She never gave in to illness or sadness and found solutions to all her problems without asking for help or advise. It wasn't because of any superiority complex, it was purely and simply a survival instinct. I had no idea whether anything had happened to her in her life to bring this about, I just knew instinctively that this was the kind of person she was and, as trying as it could be sometimes, I couldn't help admiring her for it.

For this reason, I didn't harp on about the fact that even the most able bodied person would have found it considerably difficult to balance on a pouffe balanced on an armchair, instead I set about trying to solve the problem of her imaginary gap in the curtains and came up with a plan. What I'd do, I suggested, was sew some strips of Velcro on the reverse sides of the centre edges and in future make sure the curtains were drawn with the Velcro stuck together before we said goodnight. She'd never heard of Velcro, but thought it was a marvellous idea once I'd explained it to her and she enthusiastically related the good news to Wanty Wanty when he served her tea.   "Thank you both...you know what you're doing alright...I should know...I've done it all in my time...my folk'll tell you...can't do it so much now though...not with my bad leg, ooh jibber, it does give me gyp..."

As she chattered on in her usual way, two things occurred to me. Firstly that she may well have been pegging her curtains together since day one and we'd never known about it, because she miraculously hadn't fallen and had undone them before we took early morning tea in. Secondly that it was very possible her routine had been put out of kilter by the arrival of an unexpected new face in the home (that of Miss Older) and this had caused her to feel unsettled, possibly explaining the reason for barricading of the door.

We kept her company for a little while and, at Wanty Wanty's suggestion, she let us help her onto her bed to catch up with some sleep. Never having accepted help before, this was a major breakthrough and it opened the door for us (honestly that's not intended as a pun) to get more involved with her and give her a much easier, more comfortable life from then on.

Going back to bed wasn't an option for us and after a nice big mug of coffee we got ourselves ready for work and made an early start. Luckily it turned out to be a lovely quiet Easter Sunday with no visitors, alarm bells, call bells or unexpected events of any kind. The Velcro on the curtains was a resounding success and Percy's unfortunate experience of being trapped in a room with no cat flap had no visible effect on him.

"I'm not very fond of cats," volunteered Miss Older when we were smoking our usual cigarette in the evening and I told her about the incident "they're too sneaky for my liking." She paused for a while as if assessing the possible impact of her statement, then added apologetically,

"I hope you're not offended Soneea."

"Not at all" I reassured her cheerfully. "Wanty Wanty can't stand them either. Or dogs for that matter!"

"There's more to him than meets the eye," she asserted with relief "I'm getting to know you both now, aren't I dear?"

"Mm." I responded pensively. "Do you know what else he can't stand?"

She shook her head.

"Smokers!" I revealed, which was quite true and she was tickled pink.

Chapter 31

Being called upon at night was probably the worst aspect of running the rest home and for me personally, not simply in terms of the physical discomfort either. What I hated more than anything was the intrusion and the invasion of privacy, mainly because I had a real hang-up about going anywhere at all with messy hair and no make up. It was hardly plausible or indeed appropriate to sort my hair out and slap a bit of lipstick on before responding to a possible emergency, but then I've always believed that my hang-up helped me to identify in some small way with the residents, specifically in terms of the way they must surely have felt upon losing their homes and kissing their privacy goodbye for ever.

Actually, being disturbed at night was probably the worst aspect of living in a home from the residents point of view as well, not that it happened very often, but we did tend to have spates of it when somebody was ill or there was a newcomer. Luckily, it was highly unlikely that anybody except ourselves would have heard Florence that particular night with her room situated as it was above the kitchen and next to the bathroom out of earshot, although there were times, especially when the bell was rung that the others, or at least those who weren't deaf, might be disturbed. On the whole, residents who were happy and settled were reluctant to ring the bell in the middle of the night, unless it was absolutely unavoidable.

The call bell system we inherited with the property was of the type with push buttons attached to cords, which hung either from the ceiling or the wall in the vicinity of the eight beds and the two loos. The main console with a display panel for the bell numbers was situated downstairs near that of the fire alarm and there was a bell extension to the upstairs landing as well as to the kitchen. The bell would ring for as long as the push button was depressed and it would stop ringing when it was released, thus it was possible to recognize individual ring types. For example, 'dring, dring, dring, dring,

dring, dring, dring, dring dring dring" would be Edith and 'driiiiiiig, driiiiiiig' Mrs Swain, whereas a plain 'dring' would be the Captain. Also, if one of us answered the bell and found we needed another pair of hands when we got to the caller, we'd ring twice in quick succession to alert the other person on duty. The number being rung would 'click' down on the panel and the person answering would 'click' the number back up.

It was a perfectly decent system, it had absolutely nothing wrong with it in any way at all, it was in fact the only useful piece of equipment Spit and Gob left us and, on the very rare occasion that the wiring in a push button became faulty, it was child's play to fix, even for me. Nevertheless the registration authority, in its infinite wisdom and 'one fits all' policy, would eventually make it compulsory for us to have the whole thing ripped out, shoved into land-fill and replaced with a very expensive state of the art digital variety, whose main feature was an irritating, very loud buzzer which sounded continuously and could only be silenced when one of us reached the caller and turned it off at source.

There would be no more individual ring types or coded messages, very little chance of the residents sleeping through the wretched noise it made and no way any faults could be investigated by anybody other than a fully qualified electrical engineer. Brilliant, that's progress for you.

Chapter 32

Come rain or shine, every single day of the year, it was imperative to do at least one machine load of washing, otherwise the home was guaranteed to descend into a state of chaos with serious shortages of both linen and key items of resident's clothing. In any case, it paid to stay ahead of the game to pre-empt the many unforeseeable events such as, incidentally, the addition of Miss Older's laundry that particular weekend.

Inspired by the local hardware shop, which used every tiny nook and cranny to display hundreds of goods in a relatively small area, we fixed some concertina type laundry airers from the ceiling in the utility room, where the combination of heat from the boiler and fresh air from the permanently opened louvre glass window ensured that each load dried over night and was ready for ironing the following morning.

It was precisely the ironing I was ploughing my way through on Monday morning, when the phone rang and somebody simultaneously knocked on the front door of the owners' extension, not far from where I was standing in my usual corner between the closed utility room door and the office desk, the availability of space being at more of a premium than the hardware shop could even begin to imagine. The ironing board honestly only fitted in if it was placed with the 'thin end' up against the back of the units sectioning off the food preparation area and the 'iron-rest end' against the desk directly in line with the phone. Not only did this result in me being trapped in a small space, but in Wanty Wanty living in constant fear of the phone ringing and me putting the hot iron to my ear by mistake. When I remembered to, I'd usually take the phone off the base unit and put it on the kitchen table, as indeed was the case this time and, because Wanty Wanty and Tess were both upstairs collecting the breakfast trays, I ended up getting myself into a right two and eight when I struggled to unplug the iron, extricate myself from the trailing flex, push the ironing board forwards to let me by, push it back again to clear the gangway, grab the phone and rush out of the kitchen into the extension.

"Could you hold the line for a moment please" I panted into the phone on my way and I opened the door rather more flustered and red in the face than I would have liked.

"Is that you Maud?" shouted the voice into my ear and, at the same time as I tried to say it wasn't "Can you hear me Maud? Is that you Maud?"

My great friend Danni, who I'll tell you about in a minute, smiled knowingly and stepped inside. The voice on the phone was that of an elderly lady, who's daughter Maud evidently had a similar phone number to ours. She'd misdialled it that often, she'd become an intrinsic part of our daily life to the point where we'd start to worry about her when we hadn't heard from her for a while.

"I'm afraid you've got the wrong number." I articulated into the mouthpiece clearly, slowly and loudly in the usual way. Then the line went dead, again in the usual way.

"You've got the patience of a saint" chuckled Danni, as I put the phone down gritting my teeth and went back to my corner behind the ironing board.

Danni was a very attractive, well-presented, local young mum, who'd become a really good friend after meeting us on the street the day the new sign went up. We were dead chuffed with the ingenuity of our subtle name change, especially the ivy plants to go with it, and were standing outside the property admiring the wooden board inscribed in curly Edwardian script, hanging from the black wrought iron frame with scrolled details all around the edges, when she walked by and stopped to chat.

She knew a great deal about rest homes, having trained to managerial level in a group owned by a well-known charitable organization before she got married. She'd resigned from her post, because she objected to the large extensions planned for each of the six homes belonging to the group, which already catered for over fifty, what they called, 'clients'.

Just like us, she hated the lack of domesticity typical of larger establishments, she hated the comings and goings of unfamiliar faces, the permanent staffing problems, the amount of paperwork and the large number of maintenance and cleaning personnel, to name just a few things and, just like us, she held the view that the only way to achieve high standards of personal care and offer a good quality of life was in small units with a strict maximum of ten residents.

Needless to say, we hit it off instantly and had loads to talk about. The next time we saw her, she asked if she could see the inside of the home and we were more than pleased to invite her in for coffee. In time, she began to pop in occasionally and get to know the residents and routine. When we were finally able to afford to have a day off and employ somebody, we asked her if she'd like the job, hence she was the person covering for Wanty Wanty on Tuesdays and me on Wednesdays.

As I got stuck back into the ironing, I could tell at a glance that Danni wasn't stopping. She didn't undo her coat for one thing and she didn't put the kettle on, as she normally did when she popped in, for another. Something in her expression told me she wanted to say something she thought I might not like to hear. She seemed a little awkward and my instincts told me she was probably hoping not to work that week, but didn't know how to tell me. Luckily, Wanty Wanty made a sudden noisy entrance with an armload of trays stacked with wobbling crockery and saved her the trouble.

"Don't you worry about us poor bastards working our guts out, just you stand around and enjoy life, why don't you" he began breezily, heading in the general direction of the sink "It's not enough for you to do a paltry two day week, you have to come and rub it in, watching us suffer, don't you? Thanks a lot."

This gave Danni the giggles and the confidence to tell us that she and her husband thought they might take the family to visit her sister for the rest of the Easter week, as long as it didn't put us out. We were far too easy going to let anything so trivial put us out and in any case we did have Tess on duty all week, so she was able to go without a guilty conscience.

Danni was one of the first people to tell us what was common   knowledge in the business about owner/occupier married couples, which was that they invariably ended in divorce in a very short space of time with one, or often both of them, either having a nervous breakdown, turning into a serial adulterer or becoming a raving alcoholic. Many a doctor, social worker, nurse and solicitor offered us the same information time and time again and I'm happy, no I'm *proud* to say that more than twenty years later we proved to be the exception to the rule.

Well…we're still married!

Chapter 33

Miss Older made no secret of the fact that she was relieved my day off had gone out the window, but then she hadn't met Danni yet and I was quite sure she'd feel differently when she had.

"You get very selfish when you get old" she said, by way of an apology. Coffee had been served and I was sitting with her for our usual morning ciggy, having finished and delivered the ironing.

"I hope you're not too disappointed dear," she added, tapping her cigarette into the ashtray, awkwardly with her left hand.

"Well, I *had* been hoping to concentrate on getting you registered with a doctor as well as speaking with your solicitor *and* booking a home visit with the hearing aid man, if you must know." I informed her and as I did, I caught sight of the state of her fingernails, which I'd noticed earlier were in desperate need of a manicure and I'd completely forgotten about.

"Don't bother yourself too much Soneea, I don't want to be any trouble. I've been without a doctor for so long, another few days isn't going to make any difference." As sweet as this was, she was missing the point slightly and had evidently forgotten how close Friday was.

"Listen" I said, pulling her leg "The sooner I get you sorted out with a doctor and a proper support system, the sooner I can send you home and get you out of my hair, if that's alright with you!"

"Laughter is the best medicine." she remarked, breaking into a grin "I don't need a doctor for that, I've got you!"

Louise was in her usual chair, in a world of her own, gazing out into the garden while she waited for her coffee to cool down and the Captain was standing by the dining room table, holding his already half empty cup and checking the headlines of his folded newspaper, swaying to and fro, as was his wont.

I put my cigarette out and went to get my manicure set from the utility room, leaving Miss Older to take her last few puffs and as I passed Louise, whose manners you remember were always impeccable when she was in company, a large lump of soggy crumbs from the dunked chocolate biscuit she was holding elegantly in her fingers, suddenly dropped, hit the rim of her cup and started to trickle slowly down the outside. I knew she wouldn't want any attention drawn to the fact and I pretended not to notice, as she demurely placed the remaining portion in her mouth and dabbed her lips with a napkin.

On my return however, the weirdest thing happened. Holding the cup in one hand, she started to wipe the apparently irresistible chocolate off with the forefinger of the other, licking it clean between wipes. It was the most uncharacteristic behaviour and I again pretended not to notice, going straight back to my seat next to Miss Older, who gave me a knowing glance. I picked up a nail file and took hold of her left hand, but within seconds, we were both drawn into watching Louise, who was so engrossed in her task, she began to tilt the cup more and more until in the end the coffee spilled onto the saucer and all over her book with no front cover. We both saw it coming, we both knew not to say anything and we both gripped each other's hand in an automatic helpless reaction.

"I'll just *clip* the ones on your right hand." I said, as if I'd been minding my own business "It might be a bit painful if I try to file them, don't you think?

"Mm" agreed Miss Older, still mesmerized by Louise's behaviour.

"I alway*sh* have MY nail*sh* done at the hairdre*shersh sh*alon." boasted Louise unexpectedly, a blatant lie Miss Older probably wouldn't have heard. Then she spread her hands out and admired them, suddenly becoming part of the real world, apart from the new speech impediment, which I took to be the result of biscuit stuck in her dentures, influenced as I was by the recent incident with Mrs Morris and the toffee. Then she mopped up the coffee with her napkin, which she squashed tightly into her cup on completion of the task.

116

Soon enough Tess came through from the kitchen for the cups and when she saw that I was still in the lounge, she knew to leave the tray on the table and collect the upstairs lot, leaving me to do the downstairs, so I picked up the Captain's and Miss Older's empties and approached Louise's cup last, smiling as nonchalantly as I could. When I reached for it however, she looked up at me, all red in the face and gave me the strangest, tightest grimace, her top lip disappearing completely into her mouth as if she was really cross with me for some reason. I felt quite put out, to be honest. I mean, I'd been so careful not to undermine her and this seemed no way to repay me. It was sad that her self-imposed pretentiousness could cause her to feel humiliated enough to be blatantly bitter towards me, a completely innocent person. It made me feel sad, it really did.

I tidied away the manicure set and hung up the washing in the utility room, thinking about the complexity of the human condition, leaving Tess to wash up and Wanty Wanty to work his magic on the Bernard Mathews Turkey Roll.

All of a sudden, Tess, who'd pulled Louise's squashed up napkin out of the cup, shrieked unexpectedly,

" Yuck! Disgusting! Somebody's false teeth!"

Poor Louise. She hadn't been cross with me at all. She was just trying to disguise the fact that her top denture had fallen out, presumably the real reason for her sudden speech defect. Exactly why it had fallen out eluded me at this juncture, although I did feel guilty about erroneously jumping to a rather judgemental conclusion.

I waited until it was time for the pre-lunch 'loo-run' before giving Louise her choppers back, coaxing her into her room to get to the mirror on her wardrobe door and I didn't notice anything wrong with her until we got as far as the chair lift.

Normally with Louise, who didn't particularly like to link arms or be touched at all, you'd walk beside her and show her the way by holding your hand out like a waiter in a posh restaurant and you'd stand beside the chair, or whatever you were trying to direct her to, and either pat it or wave slightly

117

along the surface if it. She'd easily get the message, even when you made some polite conversation while you were doing it. Except of course this time because, in the few seconds it took to stand beside the chair lift and wave my hand over the seat, she walked up to it, turned round and dropped herself unexpectedly into the sitting position with a loud thud onto the bottom step of the staircase.

It wasn't like she'd fallen, it was more like she'd had one over the eight and had misjudged the height and distance altogether. Not that this has ever happened to me you understand.

I switched the chair lift off at the mains, folding the arms, the seat and the foot-rest back and sat down beside her, holding on to her. Then I called out to Mrs Swain, who was right in front of us in her usual place in room three with her door open, and asked her to ring the emergency bell tied round the arm of her chair.

"Tsk…I can't get a minute's rest," she complained with her usual extraordinary wit, but I didn't have time to laugh, because Wanty Wanty appeared almost as soon as she let go of the bell.

Together we got Louise onto the chairlift and into the loo. Then we took her to her room and sat with her for a while to see what we could find out.

We needed to determine whether she had a head-ache, ear-ache, rash, sore throat, tummy-ache, runny nose, blocked nose, or any other obvious symptom and while we were getting this information, her top denture began to work itself loose again and she began to talk gibberish, which alerted us to the fact that she'd either developed a high temperature, or she'd suffered a stroke, in our experience the two most likely possibilities in the case of an elderly dementia sufferer.

Wanty Wanty went off to get a thermometer from the medicine cabinet leaving me to hold her hand and offer some comforting words. Soon enough we discovered that she did indeed have a high temperature, but we didn't think her condition was severe enough to warrant calling a doctor out on a bank holiday. We'd give her plenty of liquids and something to keep her temperature down until the morning.

When I tucked Miss Older and Mrs Swain in later that evening, they both expressed their concern about Louise and I brought them up to speed.

"Has she got a nice doctor?" enquired Miss Older.

"They're all nice at our local practise." I assured her.

"Perhaps he'd like to take me on, save me going to the surgery." she suggested.

"What a good idea" enthused Mrs Swain "Kill two Old Birds with one stone."

"That's right dear," replied Miss Older, blissfully oblivious to the remark and she reached over to her bedside table "There we are. Torch, tissues and wristwatch, all ready for use…"

Chapter 34

We made it our business to build good working relationships with all the G.P.s we came into contact with, as well as with the Consultants and other medical specialists. Either Wanty Wanty or I took residents to appointments, whenever they were well enough, and recorded them accordingly. In the case of a home visit being necessary, we made sure that the patient's details and drugs' list were at hand and we treated whichever doctor happened to call with the utmost respect, remembering as soon as we opened the door, to thank him or her for coming. We were absolutely convinced that it didn't cost anything to be pleasant and that a good reputation not only reaped many benefits, but was a better investment than any form of advertising.

To prove my point, when I rang the surgery on Tuesday morning to ask for a home visit, the receptionist knew who I was and accepted without question my judgement that it was necessary. Furthermore, when Doctor Watson, our favourite G.P., arrived in the afternoon, he walked along the hall towards Louise's room and asked if we had a vacancy for a patient of his who wasn't managing very well since his wife had been sectioned some years earlier.

"Good homes like yours are few and far between," he observed, when I apologized for being full up.

"I'll tell him to come and see you. He doesn't live far. Maybe he can go on your waiting list."

See what I mean?

After seeing Louise, he diagnosed a possible urinary tract infection. We'd need to get a sample to the surgery as soon as possible, keep her temperature down and give her plenty of fluids, ring in at the end of the week and, if the test proved positive, collect a prescription for antibiotics.

Miss Older was the only one in the lounge and he sat next to her as if he had all the time in the world. He asked her one or two questions and when she started telling him what had happened, I slipped into the kitchen for a minute or two to give her a bit of privacy. When I returned he was examining her ears in case they were blocked with wax, a possible contributory factor to her deafness.

"I was going to ask Miss Older," I informed him at a deliberately lower speed and higher volume than normal, so that she could hear too "whether she'd like to come here on a daily basis and go home at night. We could collect her and take her back every day until she's back to normal."

Miss Older's face lit up when he said he had nothing against the idea and she pointed to the window to show him where her bungalow was, just behind the fence the other side of the garage. After handing me a prescription for eardrops, he went round the whole home to say hello to the other residents, which went a long way in helping them to feel that they were in good hands and me to feel we were doing something right.

Armed with her doctor's approval of the day care offer, I dialled Miss Older's solicitor's number only to find that he'd stopped practicing ten years before the receptionist who answered the phone had even started working for the company! She promised she would get back to me as soon as she'd established which of the partners had taken Miss Older on and she suggested I check whether or not she'd received a notification letter, which was their normal procedure.

With it being Wanty Wanty's usual day off, Tess was doing all the catering tasks, I was doing all the caring ones and Wanty Wanty was on call for emergencies only, so there was no way I had time to sit with Miss Older for a ciggy all day, but I did manage to tell her about her solicitor.

"I'm not surprised he's gone, dear. He was quite old when I bought the bungalow twenty odd years ago. That was the last time I saw him." Then she found the letter she'd forgotten she received, behind her pension book in the pile of documents in her bag.

" I don't use a solicitor, unless I have to. They're all crooks dear. I shouldn't bother if I were you."

121

I phoned the duty officer at the registration unit to ask about any rules relating to day care and was told that it was acceptable for a home of our size to offer day care for a maximum of two people and, apart from the fact that I wouldn't have had time anyway, there was no point in ringing the hearing aid man until she'd had eardrops morning and night for a week.

Meanwhile Wanty Wanty was obliged to interrupt his day off and take Louise's urine sample to the surgery.

"Goodnight, Miss Older" I said at the end of what seemed like a long shift.

"Goodnight my dear, dear Soneea. Thank you so much for all you're doing. I really couldn't be luckier. I do hope you have a nice evening to yourself, you must be sick of the sight of me."

I most definitely wasn't sick of the sight of her or anybody else for that matter. I admit there were times I might feel fed up or irritated by the things residents said or did, but I honest to god was never sick of the sight of them and neither was Wanty Wanty.

Chapter 35

Normally on Wednesdays I was at college all day doing a year long course for rest home managers, designed and made mandatory by the registration authority. Naturally, there were no classes over the Easter holidays, so being on emergency duty only that particular week, was as good as having a proper day off for me.

None of the residents knew that I was attending the course on my only day off. We didn't broadcast the fact because we didn't want it to get back to the inspector, as it was against regulations not to have proper staffing levels or adequate time off between shifts. Strictly speaking, we were already in breach of the rules by having just the one day off and the only reason a blind eye was being turned, we were convinced, was because of the embarrassing amount of money and effort that had been needed for us to put Spit and Gob's disgraceful neglect right, not that it was ever mentioned, you understand.

Anyhow, it was alright for Margaret Thatcher to simultaneously run the Falklands war and the whole bloody country on a seven day week with less than four hours sleep a night *and* it was alright for junior doctors to work a seventy two hour week in N.H.S. hospitals the length and breadth of Britain. Rest home owners with a mere eight people in their care on the other hand, were treated like criminals and told they were putting vulnerable adults at risk if they worked more than fifty hours in a seven day period. (Actually I can't remember the exact figures, but it was something like that.)

It's true that we worked long hours and we worked hard, but we were really well organized and ran a very tight ship so that any one of us could take over another person's task at any time. Everything was done in a certain order and a certain way and, although there was never a time with nothing to do, it was possible for us all to take lots of short breaks, not always together, but we could take things in our stride. There was a place for everything and everything was put back in its place.

Meals, teas and coffees were always punctual and I'm absolutely certain that being in our own familiar environment helped to make the work less stressful.

I had a really pleasant Wednesday pottering about and, unlike poor Wanty Wanty, I didn't get called out to deliver or collect anything for the home, so I was as fresh as a daisy and in a really nice mood when I went back to work on Thursday morning. Until Miss Older's new solicitor got back to me, that is.

I was friendly and polite, whilst keeping myself brief and to the point about Miss Older's situation and, after establishing with me that she was compos mentis, he basically said, in a very patronizing way, that she was perfectly free to make her own decisions and could ring him or write to him herself if she wanted to. Not without sarcasm, I told him about her hearing difficulties and reminded him that she'd broken her right arm, therefore couldn't write and I explained that she'd named her solicitor as next of kin, hence it was my duty to inform him of her circumstances. I was obviously a bit peeved, but he didn't care about that at all and went on to say, in a very unpleasant tone, that if I needed to 'cover' myself, I should put it in writing for him to keep on file and abruptly wound up the conversation.

I bet you anything you like he was the type of penny-pinching solicitor who'd have had the gall to charge Miss Older for making the call. He sounded like he was, that's for sure. Miss Older had the right idea: I shouldn't have bothered with him.

Our problem, to be honest, was that it didn't seem right to be getting so involved without the backing of a third party. Stan the gardener wouldn't be back until the following Wednesday and, in any case, could hardly be responsible for her. And it wasn't just a question of needing to 'cover' ourselves, it was a question of being certain that we were acting in Miss Older's best interests, something the half-wit of a solicitor evidently couldn't give a fig about.

In the end, Wanty Wanty sat and had a long chat with her about my concerns and suggested getting in touch with the social services.

"When the doctor thinks I need a social worker, I'm sure he'll tell me," she stated decisively.

We accepted her decision, which I recorded in her notes and I didn't bother writing to the half-wit.

Chapter 36

Being far too busy and too happy with life in general to stay in a bad mood for long, we put the incident out of our minds and got on with our work.

While the residents were having lunch, we had our usual staff meeting and drew up a plan of action with our time-honoured list of things to do to set Miss Older up for day care. Apart from packing up her things, we'd need to get her permission to do an inspection of her bedroom and make sure it was safe (a risk assessment in today's lingo). Then we'd need to devise a care-plan based on her home environment and estimate how long it might take to get her up and how long to get her ready for bed.

The logistics weren't as straightforward as you might think. It obviously made sense to stick to the same routine we had at the rest home, which was to have her sit on the bed with a bowl of water on a meal trolley like the other less mobile residents, but did she have a meal trolley? Did she have a bowl, for that matter? Was she going to be safe walking to the loo during the night? Were there any dodgy looking rugs? She wouldn't have a handrail along the hall for sure and with just one arm, a walking frame would be out of the question. Would she need a commode? How long would it take to walk her to the bungalow? Did she have a spare key? What about her laundry? Would she feel we were taking over her life?

There was a lot to consider and rushing headlong into action without a plan would risk time-consuming mistakes, on top of which, failing to keep her informed might be confusing and upsetting for her.

We had our work cut out for us that afternoon, especially because unexpected tasks were tricky to accommodate under normal circumstances within the home, let alone outside and in any case, as capable as Tess may have been to be left in charge of the kitchen and the catering, she was far too young to be left on her own, even if we were only next door. So the plan was that I'd go over to the bungalow in the first instance and Wanty Wanty would go along afterwards just in case he saw something I'd missed.

Miss Older's bungalow was a perfect reflection of the straightforward, no frills type of person she was. Her furniture was solid and basic. There were no plants, ornaments, bookshelves or signs of luxury of any kind. All the floors were finished in an ordinary brown tiling, all the walls were a dull cream colour with no mirrors or pictures hanging anywhere and, apart from the large shade on the standard lamp in her bedroom, which was in a floral fabric with fringing around the bottom edge, all the soft furnishings were a tweedy sort of brown and very, very plain.

I soon established that it was too long a walk from the bedroom to the loo and that she didn't have any of the equipment she was going to need. She didn't have a meal trolley, a bowl, a commode or even a bedside lamp and I couldn't find any loo rolls in any of the cupboards after noticing the nearly empty one in her loo. Not only that, but there was no radiator in her bedroom. Fortunately I knew we had spares of everything, including a small electric fire, but my heart sank at the very thought of her spending even one night alone in such a gloomy, cold, uninviting place. The only sign of anything at all cosy was the small rug by the side of her bed and this was going to have to go, seeing as it slipped easily on the tiled flooring as soon as I put my foot on it to test it.

I opened the window and pulled down the bedclothes to let the place air. I added a couple of hot water bottles to my list and went back to the home to get everything together and put it all in the lobby. Then I decided to go and find Wanty Wanty, who was clearing out the medicine cabinet in the kitchen.

I began to tell him about my assessment and I was alright all the while we so happened not to make eye contact but, just when I got to the bit about having to remove the rug, the one and only visible piece of luxury, he happened to glance in my direction and our eyes met for a split second. It was then that a sudden surge of involuntary sadness welled up inside me, causing an incontrollable wobbling in the area of my chin and an unexpected glassy appearance over the surface of my eyes, which I was unable to hide, even though I instinctively turned away.

"What's the matter with you, you daft wotsit?" he asked, not expecting me to answer. "She likes it that way. It's her home, for god's sake."

I lit up a ciggy and pretended to start ticking things off the list while I tried to get a grip.

"I'll see if I can find one of those rubber bath mats to put under her rug, that'll stop it from slipping" said my voice and, inspired by this brilliant idea, my body stubbed the cigarette out and went off to look for one.

It didn't take that long to get everything in the kind of order we were used to, the only problem I hadn't anticipated was the shortage of power points and, with just the one double socket in the corner behind the famous chest of drawers, which was too far from the bedside table for the flex of the bedside lamp to reach, I had to make an extra trip home to get an extension lead.

In the end, by the time the curtains were drawn, the pillows were puffed up and the bedside light was on, Miss Older's bedroom didn't look bad at all. The bath mat with all its suction pads, gripped the floor beautifully and stayed hidden with no trouble under the otherwise dodgy rug and, after testing the electric heater with the door closed for a minute or two, the room warmed up really quickly. Moreover, I was absolutely convinced that Wanty Wanty wouldn't be able to think of anything at all that I hadn't already seen to. When I got back, however, he'd already thought of something that hadn't occurred to any of us.

"Have you got a telephone extension in your bedroom?" he was asking Miss Older when I walked through the lounge and for a split second I thought he'd come across an insurmountable problem.

"I've been on my own without a line in the bedroom all my adult life and never needed one, except when this happened"

she stated, lifting her plastered arm away from her body
"Anyway, I couldn't get up off the floor, so a phone wouldn't
have been much use dear."
She was right of course. We couldn't expect to cover every
possible eventuality, in any case, residents in single rooms in
all homes faced similar risks if they fell during the night and
couldn't reach a call bell.

As Wanty Wanty left the building to go and double check all
my good work in the bungalow, Florence came down on the
chairlift for afternoon tea. It was really nice to see her moving
about the place and mixing with the others, something she
never used to do when we first knew her, but it was even nicer
to see how much better she looked since I'd put the Velcro on
her curtains and she was finally getting a proper night's sleep!

"Hello there, Florence" I called up and, as she travelled
down with her right knee stretched out in the usual way, I
unfolded the walking frame, which was kept at the bottom of
the stairs especially for her, and I placed it strategically in
position for her.

"Now don't you be worrying yourself about me...I can
manage...ooh jibber...this rotten leg...you've got enough to
do...thanks all the same...I'm just going to visit my little
friend before tea."
Little friend? I thought she'd finally gone over the edge and,
not knowing quite how to respond, I just stood there with an
inane smile while she hobbled towards room three and, to my
astonishment, stopped in Mrs Swain's doorway and started
chatting to her. I had absolutely no idea she'd ever gone to
visit somebody in their room and I was thrilled to bits,
especially as I knew how much Mrs Swain loved company.
She didn't stay there for very long, but it was enough to
exchange a few pleasantries and Mrs Swain would have been
delighted.

Tess was serving the afternoon teas and I was helping
Florence to get her cushion comfortable when Wanty Wanty
came back. He sat next to Miss Older and told her that, as long
as she stayed in her bedroom until we arrived in the morning at

seven, she'd be safe. Then he told her that, although her bed at home faced west, unlike Mrs W's one, which faced east, both bedside tables were on her right hand side when lying on her back, which meant that she'd have exactly the same procedure to use the commode in her own room as she'd had in room three and wouldn't need another training session. It was a sensible enough observation and he didn't intend to be comical, but it did make me laugh and Miss Older saw the funny side as well.

"I don't know what we'd do without him, do you dear?" she chuckled and even Florence laughed at first until she cottoned on that we were talking about Miss Older going home.

"You can't be going home…not with your arm in plaster…Lordy, Lord… however will you manage?"

"I'm only going home to sleep, dear."

We left them to chat and Tess to finish serving teas and went to the kitchen to get ourselves some coffee. Everything on the list of things to do was ticked off and I was about to sit quietly and glance at the paper when Wanty Wanty unexpectedly asked whether I thought Miss Older was expecting to go home that same night. It was something that hadn't even crossed my mind as I'd simply assumed she wouldn't be going until the following day, when Mrs W was due back.

"I don't think she's in any hurry." I mumbled with a mouth full of biscuit.

"Well, we ought to give her the choice" he suggested and he opened the door and poked his head into the lounge to ask her.

" Ooh yes please!" she replied without any hesitation whatsoever.

Later that evening, when she was all tucked up in her own bed, she reached out for my hand and went through the same, by now pleasantly familiar routine,

"Goodnight Soneea and thank you, dear. I promise I won't leave this room."

Then she took her watch off and put it on the bedside table.

"There we are, torch, tissues and wristwatch, all ready for use."

And she put her head on her pillow and sighed,
"Ah, it *is* nice to be home."
Well of course she couldn't wait to get home. I knew that.

Chapter 37

I can't remember for the life of me what we did about Miss Older's early morning tea when she went back home. I'm pretty certain we wouldn't have made her a cup in her own kitchen, because it would have been impractical and time consuming to boil a kettle for just one person as well as make sure there was milk in her fridge and wash the one cup up every day. We obviously wouldn't have taken a cup with us when we went to get her up either, so I can only imagine we must have made her a flask the previous evening and put it on her bedside table. That way, she would have had a hot drink ready at any time during the night and not been tempted to get up and go and make herself one.

It's possible she didn't want a cup of tea until she got to the rest home of course, which would have been the easiest situation, but I simply can't remember anything about it. Not that you're probably particularly interested, except I do think minor details such as this might help you to get a more complete picture. One thing I do remember clearly is how unpleasant the job of looking after her between the two buildings turned out to be.

First of all, the fact that both houses were situated on a slope made the walk between the two a constant downhill, uphill, downhill, uphill affair, which was tiresome. Then, when it was cold enough to wear a coat, as it was that first Friday morning, it was a question of coat on to walk over, coat off to help her get up and dressed, coat on to walk back and coat off again, all in the space of twenty minutes. And the most tedious thing of all was the fact that the bungalow didn't lend itself to any caring tasks, particularly as it was so cold. For example, to prevent the heat from the electric fire escaping into the hall, every time anything was needed from the bathroom, the bedroom door had to be closed, which was exceptionally difficult to do whilst carrying a bowl of water.

Frankly, it was instantly clear to me that Wanty Wanty and I were going to have to take it in turns to do the job to avoid either one of us getting downright cheesed off with it. He was going to have to cover for me on my days off anyway, because Danni's shift started later in the morning and finished earlier in the evening than Miss Older needed to be collected and delivered. Thankfully, she was more than happy with whatever arrangement we proposed. It's true that she didn't have much choice, nevertheless it was obvious she wasn't simply complying, but rather was intentionally trying to make life easy for us, so she could feel as if she was making a useful contribution.

"I don't mind who comes over, dear," she assured me "as long as somebody does. Anyway you'll need a break from me, else you *will* get sick of the sight of me."

I was having this conversation with her after lunch while Tess was serving the coffees and as she was talking she appeared to be squinting and blinking an awful lot, as if she couldn't focus or something. Miss Older always wore glasses, she had separate pairs for distance and for reading and when I asked her if there was something wrong with her eyes, she said she wasn't sure and took her glasses off to have a look at them, holding them up to the light and turning them first this way and then the other. Presently, she lugged her enormous handbag onto her lap and started to dig into it.

"I get my glasses muddled up, dear" she explained, producing her other pair.

"They're the same frames. I can never tell the difference unless I put them on."

They were indeed identical, but in any case they both looked as if they'd been dipped in soup, so it wouldn't have made much difference which pair she'd put on. I couldn't believe I hadn't noticed it before and I washed them up with washing up liquid, the only possible solution.

"That *is* better." she remarked, as she tested her reading ones with her newspaper.

133

Then she tested her distance ones and afterwards, put them both back in their respective cases: the distance ones in the brown case and the reading ones in the green case.

"Gr ee n for R ee ding. You'll remember, won't you dear?" it was more of a statement than a question.

Clearly, this wasn't going to be a foolproof way of resolving the dilemma, some sort of permanent marker seemed like a better idea to me and I wandered off to the extension in search of inspiration. Soon enough, I came across some hideous green nail varnish I was quite sure I would never have actually used and I painted two little splodges on the reading glasses just inside the curvy bit for tucking behind the ear.

"There we are!" I said while I handed them back "Gr ee n for R ee ding."

She put them back in their rightful case, grinning with satisfaction and took the distance ones out of theirs and put them on.

Earlier on in the morning we'd phoned the surgery for the result of Louise's test and, being that it was positive, Wanty Wanty had gone to collect the prescription and the antibiotics. Tess had changed Mrs W's bed, replaced all her bits and pieces and given the whole room a good old spring clean into the bargain and the early morning shift had gone as smoothly as usual, although, with one resident down, we couldn't really be sure it would go as smoothly in future and just as this was going through my mind and I was looking at Miss Older's more focussed expression, thanks to the newly polished lenses in the correct glasses, Mrs W came back from her holiday.

The minute Tess answered the door, Veronica's anxious voice could be heard through the whole house, and next door for all I knew. They were late for lunch, she just knew it would happen, they'd only stopped the once to go to the loo, she'd never seen so many road works, they must have known she was coming, poor mum was starving and so on. Mrs W, on the other hand, was as placid as ever and, impervious to her daughter's panic, calmly and quietly walked into her room, took her coat off and silently started handing presents round from a plastic carrier bag: a bottle of 4711 for Mrs Swain, a can of Special Brew for the captain, a lacy hanky for Louise, a flowery notebook and matching pencil for Tess, a bottle of sherry for everybody to share and at the bottom of the bag a brand new pinny, almost exactly the same as the old one she was wearing, just not as faded, which she held up for everyone to see.

"This one's for me!" she stated, as if we didn't know.

"It's a nice green." offered Miss Older.

Every item of clothing Mrs W possessed was green. Her nighties and dressing gown, all her cardigans and dresses, her mackintosh and coat, all various shades and combinations of patterned, striped or spotted green. Even her knitted hat and gloves were green and when Wanty Wanty walked into the room from the kitchen and saw the new pinny he put his hands together and opened his mouth wide,

"What? Not another green. I don't know how you do it. So many greens in your wardrobe and not two the same. You're a genius, you really are and it's nice to have you back."

She was glad to be back and Wanty Wanty made her and Veronica a quick cheese omelette.

Chapter 38

The term 'Day Care' in rest home circles meant the provision of a safe, clean, supervised, comfortable, and stimulating environment, to include healthy food and adequate refreshments with the added availability of qualified carers for assistance in all normal tasks of every day living, from nine to five Monday to Friday, give or take. It implied the understanding that the person needing the facility was either fairly independent or had a carer during the hours before arriving and those after leaving.

There was an accepted flexibility, depending on individual circumstances, as to whether breakfast and an evening meal were part of the equation or whether the need of an assisted bath or the use of other facilities, such as hairdressing and chiropody were appropriate, but essentially it was a given that the person would arrive washed and dressed without any input from the home in question and return to their own home in the same way.

There was no expected collection and return service (sorry, that's not meant to sound like a parcel) no personal laundry or housekeeping tasks such as bed making, cleaning or shopping, no appointments, doctor's visits or transport of any description to be organized and obviously no weekends. On that basis, the term 'Half Board' was used in order to work out a recognizable fee structure and in the main, the going rate for day care was little more than half the full fee a permanent resident was charged in any given home.

In the past we'd had a lady who only came for day care on Saturdays and Sundays to give her family a break and she'd eventually died (on a week day, I hasten to add.) We'd also taken a gentleman for the odd period of a few days when his wife went away for some reason and in due course they'd moved to another area. In both cases, working out what to charge was a fairly straightforward piece of arithmetic, whereas Miss Older's particular situation didn't tick all the

136

right boxes and presented a set of criteria we'd never come across before.

We explained all this to her that Friday evening before Wanty Wanty took her home and we pointed out that, in fairness to the other residents, it seemed wrong to charge her any less than they were paying, as would normally be expected for day care, seeing as, apart from a bed for the night, she'd be getting the same help and facilities as them, if not more.

Ultimately we were in a position to charge her anything we liked and nobody would have been any the wiser, but it was precisely this aspect of her vulnerability that made us feel uncomfortable and, as you already know, the whole reason we'd made contact with her solicitor, the half wit.

As for Miss Older, she wasn't in the least bit interested in how much we were going to need to charge her,

"You're not in this for the money dear, I can see that and in any case it's not going to be for long is it?"

The meeting of the mutual admiration society that evening was spent discussing the merits or otherwise of getting in touch with the 'Registered Rest Homes Association', which we were fully paid up members of, to see whether they had any advice and in the end it was decided that I would make an informal phone call to one of the members of the committee instead, a woman called Cynthia, who'd taken me under her wing when we first joined. She was a state registered nurse with two rest homes and had suggested we meet up for lunch some day. She seemed to be extremely knowledgeable about the regulations and the politics surrounding the business and I liked her no-nonsense approach to it all. I'd ring her first thing in the morning.

At the usual time of about 10.30pm I left Wanty Wanty to do the lock-up procedure and check the downstairs residents while I went to do the upstairs lot, having suddenly remembered that I needed to get Bessie's new dress and cardigan out of the wardrobe ready for the morning.

I knew only too well that she'd want to avoid wearing them. What she'd do instead is put her usual clothes on first thing in the morning and come up with the excuse of not being able to find them or forgetting all about them if they weren't put out for her and then I'd have her daughter-in-law to contend with. Ever since we'd come to the Ivies, Bessie had only ever worn one of the same two knee-length dresses. Made from an apparently indestructible, crease resistant and stain-proof fabric, they were both cut in the same style, having long sleeves, patch pockets and zips down the front. The only difference between them was the colour and design of the cloth, one of them being chocolate brown with huge orange flowers, the other deep purple with large, lime green overlapping hoops. In the manufacturing, for some reason, even with such bold designs, no effort had been made to match up the flowers or the hoops when the back panels had been sewn to their respective fronts, hence the seams looked decidedly odd butting up against random sections of the shapes. But this was all part of their peculiar charm and in a strange endearing way they suited Bessie perfectly, as did the two cardigans she invariably wore on top: a dark brown one or a bottle green one, neither of which went with either of the dresses in any way at all.

Anyway, I helped her get her rollers in first, which she was in the middle of doing when I knocked on her door and then I got the new clothes out.

"Luver duck!" she wailed, when I took them off the hangers and put them over the back of her armchair "What's she gawn and got me this time?"

"They're very smart, Bessie" I said encouragingly. "Perfect for your 103rd."

"I'd rather go in me bleedin' birthday suit!" she grumbled. She wasn't a bad judge. The pale, striped, wishy-washy, nylon dress with no pockets just wasn't her style and as for the fluffy, baby pink cardigan, well, the less said the better!

Chapter 39

Joe the pianist had cancelled two consecutive Friday sessions because of the Easter holiday and Miss Older hadn't heard him play yet. Everybody really missed him, particularly the Captain, who always stayed in especially for him. It was the one occasion Louise, Mrs Swain and Florence never missed either, even Mrs Morris liked to be brought downstairs to join in the singalongs and you won't believe this, but whenever he played, the residents' lounge took on the exact appearance of one of those fictitious photos in care home brochures I told you about, with smiling old folk sitting around enjoying themselves. Unfortunately the room had seemed a little duller than usual during Miss Older's first week.

In all fairness to Joe, he had offered to come and play on the Saturday, the day he was due back from his holiday, to make up for his absence, but we'd tactfully turned him down so as not to upset Bessie who, as you know had an aversion to old fogies and singalongs and even though we knew full well that she wouldn't come down, we knew she'd be able to hear him in her room and it was her birthday after all.

We didn't usually buy birthday presents for the residents. What we did instead was put fresh flowers and a card on their breakfast tray, provide a cake and organize for Joe to play the piano at an afternoon tea party. In Bessie's case though, with her daughter making the cake and Joe's piano playing not being the order of the day, we felt obliged to buy her one and on this occasion, Wanty Wanty chose a book entitled '101 Clean Jokes'. He added two of his own inside the back cover and changed the title to '103 Clean Jokes', which really tickled Bessie and started the day on a good note giving us the conviction she'd be happy enough to wear her new outfit.

Tess's best friend Liz was back on duty and, after the early morning shift, which went as smoothly as the day before even with Mrs W being back and wanting a bath, Wanty Wanty and I had a lovely, full length, proper sit down breakfast with the newspapers and everything, leaving them to do all the work. Then I had a long chat with that woman from the rest homes association called Cynthia I told you about. It was nice to share ideas and experiences with somebody in the same age group and position, even if she was more experienced and more qualified than me and I agreed to meet her for a glass of wine and a sarnie in a nice pub in the town centre on my day off, but when I briefly told her about Miss Older and asked her whether she thought it was reasonable to charge her the full rate, her answer left me wishing I hadn't made the arrangement and even wandering how I could get out of it, because she told me in no uncertain terms not to get involved,

"Get the social services on to it and wash your hands of her," she practically ordered in an unnecessary, bossy way "it's not your responsibility and it'll bring you nothing but grief."

Apart from the fact that she hadn't listened to the question and had completely overstepped the mark by giving me advice I hadn't asked for, she sounded really cynical suddenly and I went right off her. It was then that I decided to stop looking for support, back up or advice of any description with regards to Miss Older's needs. Wanty Wanty and I were quite capable and trustworthy, Dr Watson was a brilliant doctor and nobody else mattered. While I'd been talking to her, the front door bell had rung and Wanty Wanty had gone to answer, so I politely wrapped up the conversation with the excuse of having to join him, which wasn't the case at all.

It turned out to be an elderly gentleman by the name of Mr Harris, who'd come to look at the home on the advice of Dr Watson. I hadn't imagined he'd come so soon and I'd forgotten to mention it to Wanty Wanty, not that it would have made any difference, seeing as they'd taken an instant liking to each other anyway and were already chatting away merrily in Mrs Swain's room when I arrived on the scene.

He was a tall, if slightly stooped, distinguished, quietly spoken man and, as well turned out as he was for a person of advancing years, I could tell that he was a little frayed around the edges and in need of a bit of T.L.C.

"You may think it a little forward of me to invite a gentleman I've only just met into my room," Mrs Swain was crooning flirtatiously "but please don't worry, I'm really quite tame. Are you staying for coffee?"

He had the sort of laugh that sounded like it needed more practice. It was too sudden somehow and too short and he seemed slightly surprised by it, as if it didn't belong to him, but he accepted the coffee offer and happily sat next to Mrs Swain in Mrs W's armchair.

"Madame, I must come clean and confess that I am already spoken for and have been tamed also, so it would seem that we are fortunately in the same boat."

Mrs Williams, in the meantime, who was sitting on the edge of her bed keeping her usual watch out of the window, suddenly pointed in the direction of the Captain in the garden,

"The Captain" she announced in her familiar monosyllabic way.

"Ah well, there'll be no hanky panky with him on board" concluded Mrs Swain and everybody laughed instantly, except Mrs Williams, who hadn't been following the conversation and had simply seen the Captain through the window.

After coffee, we took Mr Harris for a tour of the home, introducing him to the residents along the way and, although he was friendly towards everybody, he did seem a little weary, so that on the top landing outside Edith's and Mrs Morris' room, where, even with the bulky antique sideboard, there was enough room for a seating area, he couldn't resist sitting down while he told us his story.

He was a retired headmaster, his wife had been a successful theatrical costume designer and they had a married daughter and three grandchildren. Even before hitting her fifties, his wife had been diagnosed with early onset Alzheimer's disease and he'd managed to take care of her with their daughter's help well after he'd retired. Eventually though, she'd become a danger to herself and others and she'd been sectioned under the 'Mental Health Act', so he'd spent his time visiting her as often as it was allowed, even staying to feed her at mealtimes, to the point of neglecting his own needs, interests and relationships. He quite candidly admitted that it was his daughter and other relatives who were concerned, he himself was quite happy with his life and had only agreed to consider going into a home when Dr Watson had recommended it. He'd long since learnt to do all the housework, including cooking, washing and ironing and was more than capable of looking after himself, in fact being busy all the time stopped him from worrying about his wife.

It was a heartbreaking story, yet he told it with such an objective clarity, you didn't feel sorry for him, you only felt admiration and it was my gut feeling that it was the first time he'd had occasion to verbalise his situation.

His next port of call was going to be lunch with his daughter and he suggested that, before putting his name on the waiting list, she'd probably want to come along to meet us and take a look as well and he'd let us know in due course.

As we walked down the stairs with him, both Wanty Wanty and I caught sight of Bessie coming out of her room.

"That looked very much like the brown dress with the big orange flowers," said Wanty Wanty and, after seeing Mr Harris out we went back up to investigate.

"What's it got to do with anybody what I wear?" she complained bitterly when we confirmed that it was indeed the brown dress and reminded her what she was supposed to be wearing.

"I'll get the same ticking off as last year," I reminded her, in the hope that she'd want to spare me from the same fate.

"Tell her to wear it herself, if she likes it so much" she proposed instead and, catching Wanty Wanty holding the dress up to himself, waving his wrist about and pouting, she burst into a fit of laughter and that was the end of the subject.

Later that afternoon, the daughter-in-law came straight down to the kitchen to demand why Bessie wasn't wearing the planned ensemble,

"Have you tried asking *her*?" I decided to say, without being tactful and apologetic like I'd been the previous year, and then I just told her the truth,

"Our priority is to meet the needs of our residents and their choice of clothing is one of the most basic."

This shut her up and she was as sweet as pie from that point on.

Chapter 40

I'm ashamed to confess that I found it an absolute doddle to look after Louise when she was ill compared to when she was well for the simple reason that she was more compliant. To be more specific, when she needed help with absolutely every single thing, she fell off her pedestal and became a much nicer, more grateful person so that there was more job satisfaction and a more pleasant working atmosphere too. It was a stroke of luck therefore, that she was unwell during the first few days of us getting into the swing of Miss Older's new routine, which isn't a very nice thing to say, but frankly we wouldn't have coped so well otherwise.

The main problem with Louise was that she was at her most difficult both first thing in the morning and last thing in the evening, making it impossible to get into any particular routine. Some mornings she was already up and dressed when we took early morning tea in and she'd insist, for example, that she'd had a proper wash etc. even when her flannel, soap and sink were obviously bone dry. Other mornings she'd refuse to get up at all, which in itself wouldn't have really mattered, but the longer she stayed in bed, the more likely it was that she'd wet it. Similar circumstances occurred when helping her to get ready for bed in the evening so, had she been her usual self, collecting and delivering Miss Older punctually and without too much stress might not have been so straightforward a task.

In case you were wondering about Louise's bladder issues, by the way, when it came to incontinence supplies back then in the mid eighties, rest homes in our area were at the mercy of their district nurse, who ultimately decided whether or not a given resident was actually incontinent and whether or not he or she was entitled to NHS incontinence supplies.

Our own district nurse, Nurse Claire, who otherwise seemed a perfectly decent individual, suddenly began to behave like a thuggish bouncer in a dodgy nightclub when any threat was made to the size of her stock, which she guarded jealously, as if she'd dug up every single pad, bed sheet and pair of plastic pants with her own bare hands in the goldfields of the Klondike. This fact, incidentally, earned her the nickname Klondike Claire. Needless to say, her assessment concluded that Louise was *not* clinically incontinent and therefore she did *not* need incontinence supplies, just extra supervision and more frequent 'toileting' and it was because of this that we were obliged to keep a constant, vigilant eye on Louise and her waterworks.

Another thing Louise had started to do more and more was to empty the contents of her wardrobe, bedside table, chest of drawers and vanity unit, piling everything up on her bed and armchair, presumably for the same unfathomable reason she emptied her handbag in the lounge. Also she'd occasionally get undressed in the middle of the day or night and sit naked in her chair wrapped in her spare blanket or she'd unmake the whole bed taking the pillowcases off as well and leave them in a pile on the floor. Other times she'd rub all the furniture down with talcum powder. In fact there was no telling what she'd get up to when she was on her own and whatever it was took a lot of time and a lot of patience to keep putting right.

"She's obviously bored. You need to keep her more entertained" clever clogs Klondike Claire had pontificated, as if we hadn't already tried jigsaw puzzles, crossword puzzles, dominoes, card games, board games, magazines, flower arranging, knitting, crochet, charades, I spy games, performances by local theatre groups, ballet schools, choirs, etcetera, etcetera.

Anyway, while we were having another unusually long breakfast on Sunday, we thought we'd update all the care plans, something we did as and when we thought necessary and we had a long talk about the two residents whose needs had changed the most. One of these just so happened to be Louise and the other one was Mrs Morris. Louise because her mental health had obviously deteriorated substantially, as it was bound to, and Mrs Morris because her physical

145

impairments had, in stark contrast, improved greatly since we'd taken charge when, if you remember, she was slumped in her armchair unable to sit up straight following a stroke.

Just as a matter of interest, it was while Wanty Wanty and Mr Halliday were unloading the borrowed beds on our very first day that I realised Mrs Morris' condition was more to do with neglect than the severity of the stroke. I'd gone to collect the empty coffee cups, when I found her slumped asleep once again with her cup still half full. Having failed to get her to hear me, I knelt on the floor and started patting and shaking her hand until she responded, reluctantly at first, but eventually opening her weary eyes and gazing an expressionless gaze until I held up the cup and pointed, first at it and then at her, lifting my eyebrows as if in question. That's when she shook her head a bit and said what sounded like she couldn't seem to stay awake.

As you already know, there was no information on the pathetic bits of paper Spit and Gob left us as to whether she was on any medication, wore glasses, had a hearing aid or anything else about her and, although in due course we'd obviously make contact with her family, her GP and so on, my immediate reaction was to look through her belongings to get some clues. After a short search, her handbag turned up in the bottom of her wardrobe and I put it on her meal trolley in place of her cup and opened it in front of her.

Like Miss Older, she had two pairs of glasses and like Miss Older, she'd evidently dropped them in soup. With there being no sinks in the rooms, I had to take them to the bathroom to get them washed, then I got her to straighten her head and I put one of the pairs on her. There was an address book in the bag, which I held open as if for her to read and she nodded just enough to make me understand that she had the reading ones on. Using the same principle, I put the other pair on her and walked back a bit. She nodded again so as to let me know these were for distance. To prove that I'd got the message and to have a bit of fun, I kept on walking further and further back until I brought a definite smile to her face, which opened the floodgates, encouraging her to try and communicate with me.

The simple fact that she was interested in what was going on, gave her the will power to stay awake and she soon plunged her right hand into her bag as if searching for something, all the while gradually leaning back over to her left, with her left hand lying limply on her lap. Going to the rescue, I took one thing out at a time until I produced a pen, which she reached for and handed straight back. Understanding her suggestion, I started writing on the top line of an empty page in the Z section: *Hello, I'm Sonia, the new owner*. She wrote back *Thank the Lord*, then I wrote *My other half's unloading new beds* and she just pointed to what she'd already written which made us both laugh.

In this way, I found out that she'd been deaf before the stroke; that her hearing aid was in a black box in her toilet bag; that it was broken and that she was completely cut off without it. Having located the hearing aid, the only thing wrong was that the tube, which normally connects the earpiece to the amplifier, had come away and the apparatus itself had been left in the 'on' position and completely drained the battery. As was common, the spare batteries were underneath a removable felt partition in the bottom of the box and I soon had it up and running. On hearing a human voice the first time in God knows how long, she didn't know whether to laugh or cry.

Bit by bit over the very first week she began to regain some of her speech and, as we got used to it, we learned all about the horrendous things Spit and Gob put her through. For one thing, they lost their temper with her when she fell out of bed during the night and woke them up and, even though she couldn't hear what they said, they scared the life out of her with the way they dragged her up off the floor shouting in her face. It happened more than once to the point that she became too scared to go to sleep and lay awake hour after hour wishing she could die. Then, when she tried to stand up by herself one time, she was pushed back into her armchair and she knocked the side of her head on the wing. Even without her glasses on she could tell it was the husband, because he was only wearing underpants. Anyhow, that's when the hearing aid came apart and he snatched it out of her ear and shoved it in its box. She knew it was kept in the toilet bag because she'd seen it in there on Fridays, the only day they gave her a quick wash and brush up for the benefit of her sister and niece, who visited every week. She couldn't physically get it herself and she couldn't communicate its whereabouts. In any case, she was so tired from being awake all night long she spent most of their visits fast asleep.

Hard to believe, isn't it? And I could go on. There were loads of other things she told us, things we couldn't dwell on, things we tried to help her forget, things the almighty, highly qualified inspectors, with their apparent vast knowledge and lengthy experience, were obviously too bloody short sighted to notice.

Long before the end of our first year, after a lot of hard work, a bit of patience, a few setbacks, but great courage and determination on her part, she regained the strength in her neck to keep her head upright; she partially regained the use of her left hand, her speech and her balance; she rekindled her interests in sport, current affairs and romantic novels and her sister and niece's visits on Fridays became the jolliest weekly events filled with constant banter and laughter.

More recently, she improved her aim when directing cutlery to her mouth as well as her ability to chew and swallow, so that Wanty Wanty firstly stopped having to liquidise her food then stopped mashing it up and, just in the last couple of days, stopped needing to feed her as well.

So the long talk Wanty Wanty and I were having was about whether there was anything we could do A, to manage Louise's erratic behaviour in a better way and B, to improve Mrs Morris' quality of life now that she was more independent.

In Louise's case, we'd both often wondered whether she'd be less likely to do all the peculiar things she did, if she were in a sharing room with somebody watching and we knew we might have to try this eventually if we were to prove to the authorities that we were coping with her and meeting her needs, thus avoiding the awful scenario of being told to move her to an EMI home. It broke our hearts to think of Louise in a place full of people like Doris, with their clothes shrunken and all creased up, being cared for by those unglamorous carers in nylon overalls and black lace up shoes. Appearances meant so much to her, they were part of her psyche. If things looked alright, they *were* alright, if they didn't look alright, her world fell apart.

In Mrs Morris' case there was no discussion. It was plain that a single room on the ground floor would be a great improvement. It would give her more privacy when she wanted it or conversely, more contact with the other residents and the outside world.

The way forward then was quite simply for them to swap rooms, except that it was vital, as usual, to discuss the pros and cons first, rather than go full steam ahead at the risk of causing anxiety to either one of them or upsetting the equilibrium of the home.

Wanty Wanty was extremely sensitive to the feelings of all the residents and anyway never took kindly to change of any description. His opinion was that it was alright for Mrs Morris to move to a single room on the ground floor, which would be an obvious improvement, but for Louise to move to a sharing room upstairs, might not seem very positive, which he felt really bad about. Not only that, but he was worried about Edith, who could be surprisingly switched on and might object to a new roommate.

I on the other hand, had an inclination to be more detached and realistic, welcoming any change that brought practical solutions and it was my opinion that if we didn't take advantage of Louise's unusually malleable frame of mind, it would be the devil's own job to move her eventually, which we would surely have to do, aside from which, her day to day life in a sharing room would hardly change at all.

149

In the end, we both had to try and look at the situation objectively keeping the residents' best interests at heart and there was no getting away from the fact that switching rooms was the kindest and most intelligent thing to do.

Chapter 41

Whenever the front doorbell rang, Mrs W had the most annoying habit of standing right in the way to tell whoever went to answer it that it was ringing.

"Doorbell, darlin'" she'd announce every single time in exactly the same toneless voice.

For some reason, Wanty Wanty eventually learnt to mimic this to a T and whenever the opportunity presented itself, he either stood in for her, as he'd done when she was away (a detail I didn't mention because I was trying to ignore it) or he stood right beside her and repeated it after her, which could be side-splittingly funny if you were in the right frame of mind, but bloody irritating if you weren't.

I *wasn't* funny that Sunday morning around about coffee time, because I was fully preoccupied with the problem of deciding who to mention the room swap idea to first and, on my way to finish a manicure round, I'd had to do a detour to answer the front door, in itself an aggravation, so finding the two of them standing in the way saying 'doorbell darlin' like a couple of annoying minah birds, was enough to drive me to distraction and make me brush past them in a real strop. Not surprisingly therefore, I was miles away when I opened the door to Mr Harris, who'd brought his daughter to see the home, and I was noticeably slow to respond, staring blankly back at him when he made the introduction: "This is Janet" and forcing him to clarify with "My daughter". I snapped out of it apologetically and invited them in.

Mrs W had already told Mrs Swain who it was at the door and had gone back to sit by the window, leaving Wanty Wanty to behave like a grown up again and offer coffee to the unexpected visitors.

"What a lovely surprise!" came the warm, welcoming sound of Mrs Swain's voice from room three where we were standing "You couldn't keep away, could you?"

Mr Harris emitted one solitary peal of laughter as he walked into the room and all at once his daughter stepped away to stand with her back against the wall, as if trying to hide, and burst into tears.

"Oh come on!" remarked Wanty Wanty. "It's not that bad a home."

"No, you don't understand" she replied wiping her eyes and laughing at the same time "It's just that I can't remember the last time I saw him laugh. I thought he'd forgotten how to." And it all came pouring out. The years of stress her mother's illness had caused, the constant grieving in spite of there not being a death, the sense of guilt at enjoying anything at all, the helplessness and on top of all that, her own personal agony having to watch her father devote so much time and energy, at the expense of his own welfare, to the woman he'd always loved, the woman who no longer even recognised him.

We led her through to the lounge, where Miss Older and Florence were already having their coffee. She said she didn't need to look round the rest of the place, she wanted to put her father on the waiting list anyway, because she could tell it was the perfect environment for him and she began to make small talk with the Captain who'd come in because it had started to rain. A lively conversation ensued, with every body joining in, and when she found out that Miss Older lived next door and was going home at night, I saw her eyes light up and that's how I knew that soon enough Mr Harris would become our second day care resident.

Chapter 42

The remaining five weeks of Miss Older's time with the plaster cast on her arm seemed to fly by as we settled into a new kind of normality and her broken bone quietly got on with the business of healing.

Mrs Morris and Louise swapped rooms; Miss Older met Danni and liked her very much; Stan the gardener came back from his holiday; Joe the pianist did his usual Friday stints; Louise made a full recovery from her infection and Mr Harris formally took up day care for a trial period of a month.

I met Cynthia for lunch as planned and ended up having a surprisingly pleasant time. She was good company and didn't talk shop as I'd anticipated, instead she talked about her NEW CAR, her husband, her staff, her NEW CAR, her hobbies, her education, her NEW CAR, her friends, her holiday plans, her NEW CAR, herself, herself and her NEW CAR again. I could hardly get a word in, but I actually didn't mind, because she was very entertaining in spite of it and a welcome distraction from what had become my everyday life with needy elderly people, doctors, nurses, loo runs, regulations, bums and commodes.

More than anything else, I was dead pleased she didn't bring up the subject of Miss Older, because I wasn't sure how she'd react to me ignoring her advice. What she did do, was give me the distinct impression she'd completely forgotten about our entire telephone conversation by telling me a few things I already knew, which she couldn't possibly have told me any other time.

There'd be an extraordinary meeting of the association on the subject of the new regulations and we knew we'd see each other then, but we arranged to have lunch together again, once my college course was over and I got my Wednesdays back, sometime in June and we parted company on a really friendly note.

Danni, who got on very well with Miss Older, was impressed with the success of the room swap, in particular the attention we paid to putting Louise's and Mrs Morris' personal belongings in exactly the same places they'd been kept in their old rooms down to the tiniest detail and also the fact that we'd even switched the pictures on the walls over, so that both residents would feel they were in truly familiar surroundings. It occurred to her that all the furnishings and fittings were the same in both rooms, an unexpected bonus in what was after all an unforeseen circumstance. I thought this was a really clever observation, although to be honest I did swap the bedside tables over, because they had different drawer arrangements.

We couldn't be sure how Louise would behave in the long term, but we noticed that she didn't recognise her old room when walking past it, or even go up to her new room by herself for that matter and everybody agreed that Mrs Morris had a new lease of life, being so close to the lounge and able to come and go independently. Best of all, when she was in her room, she liked to sit with her door open and see people coming and going, which she couldn't do before. As for Edith, nobody could tell whether she was truly happy with her new roommate or merely going through an unusually extended sweetness and smiles stage, but we were confident that if she were to go through one of her spates of abusive ramblings, she wasn't going to be a threat to anybody, because she was chair-bound and always had one of us with her when she was moving about.

When Stan visited Miss Older after doing her gardening, he was visibly surprised to find her looking so well, which was good news, being that he was the only person who knew how she looked before she came to us.

Interestingly, excluding any actual physical illness to deal with, when it came to making a resident *look* better as well as *feel* better or vice versa, the two were inherently connected to each other in such a way that it was hard to know which to aim for first. In any case, either one would follow the other with equal certainty in every case.

As far as we were concerned, to achieve success in both objectives, it was crucial not only to do the glaringly obvious of sticking to a proper routine, administering all the medication correctly and making sure people were comfortable and so on, but also to pay attention to all the little things in life. Therefore manicures were done on a weekly basis and included the offer of applying moisturiser to hands and face, removing unwanted whiskers and trimming eyebrows; hearing aids and watches were kept in good working order; spectacles were cleaned and residents were helped to wash underarms and private parts on a daily basis; those with difficulty bending over or leaning back into a sink (which was all of them to be honest), got their hair washed when they were in the bath with me providing a drying and styling service for the ladies and Wanty Wanty a shave and spruce up for the gentlemen afterwards. If they couldn't manage it themselves, residents' shoes and bags were polished, missing buttons were replaced and hems that came undone were mended. All clothing was washed regularly at the recommended temperature, separately from soiled bed linen and everything was pressed beautifully before being put away.

Miss Older's improved appearance, therefore wasn't solely attributable to the obvious things you'd expect from a home, but also, or mostly I should say, to all those little things, which Joe the gardener wouldn't have actually been able to pinpoint, but his positive reaction had an instant uplifting effect on Miss Older herself, it gave all of us a sense of satisfaction and it had the effect of giving the other residents a feeling of pride, which all fed nicely into the atmosphere of general well-being we made it our business to create.

Miss Older's course of eardrops helped to remove built up wax, restoring some hearing to her right ear, but her left ear turned out not to have any hearing in it whatsoever and, even before she had the plaster cast removed, the hearing aid man came to the home, tested them both with his magic box of tricks, took a mould and produced a tailor made hearing aid which gradually, as she got used to wearing it, greatly improved her quality of life.

On Mr Harris' first day, he was so looking forward to having a bath, he arrived with a change of clothes nearly an hour before we were expecting him. After that, he arrived earlier and earlier, until we had to tell him that seven thirty was the earliest we could open up and that's what he finally stuck to. He soon lost his 'frayed round the edges' look and settled into his new routine, which made life more pleasant and more manageable for him so that, even before the month's trial was up, he made up his mind to stay on day care for good.

His daughter was pleased to see how quickly he began to look and feel better; the ladies were pleased to have a gentleman in their midst who stayed indoors for some of the time at least; Dr Watson was pleased he helped solve a problem and we were pleased that the business was going from strength to strength. In fact everybody was pleased with everything and life in general was very pleasing indeed.

Chapter 43

Sometime during those last few weeks, Miss Older received a letter from her only surviving relative, a cousin in Australia, and she asked me if I'd mind writing a letter back to him, which she would dictate. It went something like this:

Dear cousin Cyril,

Thank you for your letter. I am very glad that you are back home and feeling better after your operation. Now it is my turn as I have broken a bone in my wrist and have my right arm in plaster. What a pair we are! The nice lady, from the rest home next door I told you about, is looking after me and she is kindly writing this letter for me.

Please do not worry about me as I spend all day with her and am being well cared for. I have got a new doctor, a new hearing aid and a new appetite! It is very nice to have all my meals made for me.

That's all for now,
your cousin Ethel.

I wrote it in my neatest handwriting, yet when she changed her spectacles to read it back to me, I was surprised at the apparent trouble she was having deciphering it and, since her reading glasses were still clean from when I'd literally washed them up, it suddenly occurred to me that she was probably well overdue for an eye test.

Looking back and thinking about it now, I can't for the life of me work out why this wasn't blatantly obvious to me from the start. She hadn't seen a doctor, district nurse, social worker, chiropodist or solicitor for years and an optician was hardly likely to be on her list of priorities. So, just when I was thinking that her physical needs were going to be all sorted out before she went back to the bungalow on a full time basis, which seemed to me to be our responsibility, here was another fairly important matter that couldn't be ignored

As callous as this may sound, I didn't want to feel obliged to take her to appointments or be responsible for her in any way once she'd left The Ivies. I realized how difficult it was going to be for me to draw the line between friendship and a sense of obligation and in the long run she needed to be fully independent, whatever my feelings, in any case I was seriously too busy to take on any more responsibilities. Naturally, I envisaged popping over to see her or phoning her up from time to time, but that was all and at this stage Cynthia's words of warning began to ring in my ears.

In the home, we had an arrangement with a travelling optician, who offered home visits for group bookings and I'd have been more than willing to collect her for one of these, had all the residents not already been tested fairly recently with the next booking not due for well over a year. The prospect of looking for a local optician with somewhere close to park the car, making the appointment, taking her there, waiting for her, making sure she had money on her, driving her back home and then going to collect the glasses when they were ready, was far too hideous and time-consuming a task to even contemplate, especially in light of the fact that, while all this was going through my mind, Miss Older reminded me in the most glorious way how utterly trying the elderly could be when you were with them for too long with nothing to actually do.

First of all she handed me an envelope, which took her a while to separate from the pile she had in her handbag, to copy Cyril's address on, then she put the letter in it and licked the edge slowly from side to side and back again and meticulously stuck it down rubbing it over and over again while I waited. Next she took out a booklet of stamps and some airmail stickers and carefully tore off what she needed while I still waited, then she licked these fastidiously, one by one before attaching them onto the exact spot and thumping them down with her fist more fervently than was remotely necessary, causing the meal trolley to wobble uncontrollably and pushing my patience to its very limits while I continued to wait. Finally she handed it to me with a satisfied smile,

"There we are dear, one letter, all stamped and ready for posting."

Get the picture?

You can imagine my relief when I found out that regular eye tests were one thing she believed strongly in and that a reminder to make an appointment would be due in the post anytime soon, not only that, but she had a long standing arrangement with Stan the gardener who always took her and his wife on the same day, when she'd treat them both to fish and chips to eat in the car afterwards.

Phew!

Chapter 44

Miss Older's plaster finally came off. I took her to the hospital appointment myself. For physiotherapy she was given a series of exercises to do at home, in preference to further hospital appointments and, after spending a final week with us on day care, she went back home.

As much as she was genuinely missed, I can't pretend it wasn't lovely for Wanty Wanty and me not to have to do the twice daily bungalow run and we settled into another kind of normality with Mr Harris becoming as much a part of our lives as she'd been.

I kept in touch with her about once a week, not on the same day and not at the same time of day, so as to avoid turning it into a routine and to make it more of a surprise as well. Once in a while, I popped in to join her at cigarette time, but I made sure to stay away on Wednesdays, when Stan went to do the gardening, so she'd have two days of contact with the outside world as opposed to just the one. On Wanty Wanty's advice she got the GPO to install a telephone extension in her bedroom and she kept our number handy, just in case of emergencies.

In early summer I finished my college course at long last and I remember it being round about this time, when I added my certificate to the display of documents in the hall required by the registration authority, that we had our second batch of annual inspections.

Inspections were enough to drive home owners barmy and everybody in the business dreaded them, but mainly because all the inspectors were evidently trained to be as impersonal and as antagonistic as possible and to treat us all like potential criminals, with the utmost suspicion.

The health and hygiene inspector, for example, flummoxed by the spanking new kitchen and the absence of any irregularities of any kind on his first inspection the previous year, decided to get pernickety over a hairline crack in a wall tile,

"Cracked tiles such as this provide ideal breeding conditions for bacteria. It needs to be replaced as soon as possible" he cautioned with ludicrous formality.

"It's not meant to be a bloody food preparation area, for Christ's sake!" screamed Wanty Wanty when he'd gone, slapping a slice of bread on it to prove his point and later, with great relish, he set about covering the offending item with white Fablon, cut to a perfect fit, so that it looked like a brand new tile and wasn't noticed when he came back this time, or ever again, for that matter.

Similarly, the fire officer, not content with the one hour fire proof ceilings, the fire blanket in the kitchen, the self closing doors, the extinguishers and the weekly fire alarm tests, decided it would be a good idea to promote a monthly evacuation practice. I wont tell you what Wanty Wanty said about *that* idea.

When it came to the registration authority's inspection, not a word was mentioned by the Inspector (last time or this time) about the striking transformation of the entire home and everything in it, not to mention the instantly visible improvement of the residents themselves. The same pen pusher turned up both times with his massive briefcase and subjected us to the most long winded, mind numbingly boring three hour sessions of form filling you could possibly imagine, with him pontificating and lording it over us without compunction and us producing exactly the same mountain of documents and answering exactly the same long list of questions. During both inspections each room was meticulously measured from skirting board to skirting board to make sure they complied with the minimum size required by law, as if it were possible for them to have shrunk or for us to have stolen chunks to put somewhere else in the meantime.

It was so utterly exasperating that Wanty Wanty had to repeatedly leave the room under some pretext or other to stop himself from exploding with indignation.

If only the inspector's job had included doing something useful like stripping a bed, lifting the lid off a commode or opening a few cupboards, true standards could so easily have been revealed. People like us wouldn't have minded one bit and the likes of Spit and Gob wouldn't have been able to get away with their deplorable neglect.

The inspectorate seemed only to want to tick the right boxes, which in our opinion was a complete waste of everybody's time *and* our money, since we had to pay for the privilege.

Anyway, I'm not going to go on about it for the sake of making a political issue, but I simply must tell you that many a home owner actually ripped off all the skirting boards in rooms that fell short of the correct square footage after a particular inspection, so that they could tick the right box on the next inspection. Honest to God, that's what they did and guess what? The rooms then magically complied!

With regards to the new proposed regulation about the double room ratio though, there were no tricks to pull. Homes registered for less than ten were not allowed any double rooms; a ten bedded home was allowed one double room; a twenty bedded home two double rooms and so on and this inspection was the first formal verbal confirmation we received that our county was intending to implement it forthwith. It was made absolutely clear that we would not be able to keep our present registration for eight, unless we agreed to convert the two double rooms into singles, like I told you earlier.

We already knew that the income from six residents wouldn't be enough to cover our outgoings and, in any case, a reduction in the number we were registered for would automatically reduce the value of the home and put us into negative equity, so this wasn't going to be an option. The inspector knew this also and, to soften the blow, he decided to do an impromptu feasibility study of the two rooms in question, as if we hadn't already had the savvy to do one for ourselves.

Room three on the ground floor lent itself perfectly, he revealed knowingly, since the internal wall housing its present door, ran along the hall, where a second door could easily be accommodated. A stud wall down the middle of the room would produce two singles, which would more than comfortably meet the requirements.

Pure genius, don't you think?

Room six upstairs was a little more tricky, he conceded, because, in order to access the proposed second room, we'd have to lose the small loo, which was a legal requirement. Ah, but that wasn't really a problem, he discovered. All that was needed was to relocate this to the opposite side of the landing against the wall where we'd made the seating area. Simple. We didn't bother telling him it wasn't an outside wall but the shared wall between the two semis, there didn't seem to be much point.

What we were more concerned with, we explained patiently, was the fact that the stud walls were going to have to butt up against the actual glass of the bay windows and follow the shape of the window sills downwards, which we loathed the idea of with such a passion, we couldn't envisage tolerating the ensuing cheap and nasty look of the place both inside and outside, let alone trying to make people pay for it.

If his flabbergasted expression was anything to go by, he was evidently on a completely different wavelength. As far as he was concerned, he'd found a perfectly decent solution to our predicament and this appeased his conscience, allowing him to end the inspection looking positively smug on what he thought was a high note.

It was never going to be an option, not for us. What we were banking on instead was people power. There'd be objections from all over the country, we were sure, and rest home associations would get together and take it all the way to parliament. After all, the logic behind the legislation was to prevent the money making wise guys in the business from cramming as many beds as they could into homes that weren't purpose built, without due consideration to acceptable living standards. It was *not* to try and reduce beds for no apparent reason and this is why it was positively perverse for the authorities to promote the butchering of perfectly decent homes just to make them fit the bill. It simply didn't make sense and we were confident it wouldn't happen.

The mutual admiration society meeting that evening, started with some animated chat about how to become proactive and raise awareness, maybe start a petition, write to the newspapers or get in touch with a local radio station. We could organize a tea party at the local community centre, we decided. Tess and her band could perform, the residents could go and we'd soon get people on our side. But we were both so exhausted, it was hard to keep up this enthusiasm, so we shut up the shop and went to bed early.

Even talking was tiring after an inspection.

Chapter 45

The reason I remember the exact first time Miss Older rang us from the bungalow is because it was the same day we had to call out the bomb squad.... yep, that's right, the bomb squad and I thought she'd seen the commotion in the street and that was why she was ringing.

We were getting some old concrete posts dug out, which were remnants (on our side) of a defunct alleyway between the two properties. They were positioned at intervals of six feet along the far end and round the back of the extension, an area left as a building site courtesy of Spit and Gob, but a potential space for a secluded owners' garden, accessible via both the front and back door of the extension. Hidden as it was from public view, it was the last on our long list of improvements and we'd been looking forward to getting it done before Tess broke up for the summer holidays, which is how I know it would have been around about the middle of June.

The same local family run business as had renewed the outside paintwork and driveway when we first moved in agreed to take on the job and we already knew the two young workmen who turned up nice and early on what was to become a memorable Monday.

Wanty Wanty got on really well with them both and ended up spending the whole blooming morning popping in and out with cups of tea far more often than was remotely necessary and it was just after lunch that he returned unusually quickly from one of these trips looking positively panic stricken, hollering as he ran through the kitchen,

"Quick Son. (That's me. Short for Sonia.) They've found a bomb! Honestly, I heard it TICKING!"

Without conferring, we flew into emergency mode, he to grab the portable phone and start dialling the emergency services and me, for some inexplicable reason, to go out and verify his story.

"Stand AWAY from the area!" I bellowed at the two bemused workmen, shooing them away to add weight to the command, as if I were controlling a huge crowd. The fact that they were leaning on their spades, gazing into the cavity they'd been digging, looking unreasonably unperturbed at the rusty object beyond, should have told me it was just a prank and if they'd even had the slightest intention of owning up to it, as they later claimed, my ridiculously exaggerated response utterly put paid to it, assisted somewhat by Wanty Wanty appearing in the doorway with the phone to his ear giving directions to the police, who were evidently already on their way.

As soon as I witnessed the ticking, I shot back into the house and made for the residents' lounge to get everybody away from the window, which I imagined might get shattered in the event of an explosion, not that the registration authority issued any guidelines on the subject.

As expected after a meal, the Captain was already in the front garden and Florence and Mrs Morris had gone back to their rooms to watch the news, so only Mr Harris and Mrs W were in the danger zone, finishing their coffees at the table, right in front of the window, although, still in range of possible shards of flying glass, was Louise in her armchair, sorting out her handbag on the meal trolley for a change.

I was a bit more tactful this time and calmly explained why everybody needed to move to room three at the front of the building, which they accepted without question, with Louise even losing interest in both her bag and its contents and, before I'd got everybody settled, bringing Mrs Swain up to speed, the first police car was already pulling into the drive.

" Police" announced Mrs W from her usual position at the window.

I had visions of the Butch Hairdo and PC Brown ambling up to the front door with their flipping clipboard and I went through to the lobby in preparation. Instead two much more switched-on individuals were already out of the car and moving swiftly

166

past, towards the side gate, evidently being directed straight to the back by Wanty Wanty still on the phone.

At the sight of a second police car, the Captain came in to ask what was going on.

"You stay inside" he suggested confidently, when I told him. "I'll keep watch outside and send the troops through the gate." Although it seemed slightly ludicrous, he said it with a certain relaxed authority, calming my nerves considerably and I went to tell Mrs Morris she'd be safer in room three with the others, having suddenly thought that her window was just along a bit from the lounge window and just as likely to explode. In the time it took me to walk with her and get her sitting next to Louise on Mrs Swain's bed, the bomb squad had been and gone after establishing that the suspected bomb was merely a rusty old alarm clock and it was just as Wanty Wanty was telling me this in the kitchen, where I'd gone to get an update that the phone rang in his hand, making us both jump out of our skins.

"Hello, it's Miss Older. Could Sonia come please?" asked the voice without waiting for an answer and, as he playfully ushered me out of the front door of the extension I told him about the residents waiting for the all clear in room three.

Quite a crowd had gathered in the street and, as I walked down the drive, I noticed that the Captain was holding court beautifully, giving The Ivies an unexpected bit of free publicity. Miss Older would have been able to see this from her front window and when I let myself into the bungalow, I was convinced I'd find her in a panic, simply in need of some reassurance as a result. Instead I found her in her kitchen at the back of the house, oblivious to the drama outside, looking as white as a sheet, clutching her left hand close to her body wrapped in a very bloody tea cloth.

"Ooh Soneea, Soneea, I *am* sorry, dear" she sobbed, while I unravelled it "I was pressing the rubbish down into the dustbin. Ooh it does hurt! It was the corned beef tin, I think." One look at the laceration on the palm of her hand, in the fleshy bit underneath her thumb, told me she was going to

167

need stitches and after using her phone to call Wanty Wanty and grabbing a clean cloth, I drove her straight to casualty, passing the Captain and the dispersing crowd first and, further down the road, Mr Harris on his way to visit his wife in the EMI home.

It was a good three hours before I got back, during which time Wanty Wanty had collected all the empties, tackled the washing up, cleaned the kitchen, set the trays for afternoon tea, dispensed the tablets and done the 'loo run' single handed. I couldn't bear to take Miss Older back to the bungalow, as she had to have six stitches and an anti tetanus jab and was quite traumatized, so she came home with me.

"Ooh, it *is* nice to be back." she sighed, as she settled into her old chair "I'll have to come back on day care for a while, won't I dear?"
She was right of course.

Meanwhile, the two workmen had come clean about their prank and I found them standing at the back door laughing their heads off, while they explained how the whole thing had spiralled out of control when we didn't give them the chance to get a word in edgeways.

I was beside myself with anger, especially as they seemed to be boasting about it and could so easily have avoided telling us, which in fact would have been more intelligent, and I was on the verge of hurling a barrage of verbal abuse at them when Wanty Wanty, who was not in the slightest bit amused either, stopped what he was doing and interrupted me.

"Frankly" he began, in an uncharacteristic very angry tone of voice. "I don't think it was in the slightest bit funny. It was a bloody waste of public money that's what it was, not to mention my bleeding time."
And then, without meaning to be comical in any way at all, he inadvertently added:
"It was bang out of order, if you ask me."
After a moment of baffled silence, it provoked raucous laughter, even from me.

Chapter 46

Every Wednesday, when Stan used to do Miss Older's gardening, which he naturally got paid for, he used to collect her pension and do a bit of shopping for her as well. Evidently it was an arrangement that had developed over time, as she'd gradually found the weekly excursion more and more difficult to manage. Her pension was actually due on a Thursday, so she had to wait until Stan came on the Wednesday after, because it was the only day he could manage and he was her only regular visitor. He was a nice old boy, we all liked him and Miss Older often told us she didn't know how she'd have managed without him. He was reliable and trustworthy and always happy to replace a light bulb or fix a dripping tap for her, without making a song and dance about it.

To thank him for his kindness, she used to add a couple of bottles of Guinness to her shopping list and invite him to have a drink with her, not that she always drank the whole bottle, in fact I'm not sure she even liked it to be honest, but she knew it was Stan's drink and this was her way of showing him her appreciation.

While Miss Older was at the rest home, they kept up this ritual, with Stan letting himself in the back door of the bungalow to get the shopping list and the signed pension books left on the kitchen table. He'd use a key hidden in a secret place in her garden and join her in the residents' lounge at about four o'clock.

On the Wednesday of the week she cut her hand, Miss Older had the presence of mind to leave a note for Stan to tell him she was back with us on day care, as it was far too early in the morning to ring him when Wanty Wanty collected her and, in any case, she only ever used her phone for emergencies. It was after the residents' supper when I got back from whatever I was doing on my day off that I found a dear little pot plant with a card from her to thank me for taking her to hospital. She'd gone through a lot of trouble to give Stan instructions as to what sort of plant and card she wanted and she'd written a few words herself, so I was really pleased with it and I decided to join her for her evening ciggy to thank her.

She was reading her book at the time and quickly put it down when she saw me coming, in an attempt to hide a birthday card she was using as a bookmark and, as she did so, her date of birth flashed through my mind, 1/6/1897, a date I was all too familiar with from her index card, but one that hadn't actually sunk in as being the month of June, so I'd obviously missed it.

"I'm eighty seven now, dear, but I don't like birthdays much, so don't worry" she said, reading my thoughts and to get off the subject, she took her new reading glasses off, which Stan had collected and she asked me if I'd mark them with the same green nail varnish I'd used on the old ones.

"I like having the same frames for both my specs" she explained. "It's hard enough to find one pair to suit me."

After her stitches came out and she was put on the district nurse's visiting list, Miss Older went back home and our concerns about her getting lumbered with Klondyke Claire and being treated roughly by her proved to be quite unfounded, because she confided in Miss Older about her continuing disenchantment with her position and turned out to be a perfectly nice person. Her original job description was a world away from the managerial role it had mutated to, she explained, and she had to spend more and more time organizing and delegating with less and less time left for the actual nursing she'd trained for. She was often so rushed, she left her patients with the impression she was brusque and uncaring, which she regretted. Miss Older soon became fond of her and long after her hand was well and truly healed, Klondyke Claire would pop in and see her any time she came to visit a resident in the rest home.

Eventually she began to visit her whenever she was passing, often coming over for a chat with us and spending time with the other residents too. She even got to know about her nickname, which Mrs Williams blurted out by mistake one day when announcing her arrival. Wanty Wanty and I were struck dumb with embarrassment, but guess what? She turned out to be as pleased as Punch and couldn't wait to tell her superiors about it. It was definitive proof, she explained, that contrary to their accusations, she was not wasteful with the supplies they were always trying to cut back on.

Well it just shows you. Never judge a book by its cover, eh?

Chapter 47

Notice of the date and venue for the extraordinary meeting of the registered rest homes association arrived in the post before Cynthia and I got the chance to meet up for lunch and she phoned to suggest picking me up to go together since she had to pass The Ivies on her way.

To be honest, I didn't really fancy the idea because, as a committee member, she had to get there early to set up and I knew I'd get roped in to help, not only that but I'd planned to fit in some errands on my way there and on my way back. In the event I felt obliged to say yes, because she was so enthusiastic about the idea and it seemed rude to refuse.

It must have been well into July, since I clearly remember Tess being on her summer holidays and leaving her to hold the fort with Wanty Wanty, rather than getting Danni in for an extra duty.

Cynthia arrived punctually at 10am and I was waiting in the lobby so as to see her pulling up and save her getting out of the car. I'd forgotten all about her blooming car and wished to God I hadn't agreed to go with her the minute I set eyes on it again. It was th*ee* most embarrassingly flash ostentatious spanking new convertible sports car you ever did see, complete with a ridiculous personalised number plate, CYN 4U or something equally puerile and painfully inappropriate for a rest home owner. When she'd first shown it off to me, I'd had serious trouble putting the right expression on and making the right noises. I'd even felt proud for once to drive off in our humble Skoda. But this time I was actually going to have to be seen in it and, if I thought lowering my five foot nine inch frame into what turned out to be not much more than a two foot square space was the most awkward thing I'd ever done, it was only because I hadn't taken into account getting *out* of it, indeed my Lucie Clayton training in 'Getting into and out of a car in a ladylike fashion' was of no use whatsoever in either case.

At the meeting I didn't really gel with any of the other rest home owners, not that I had much time to, what with setting out the chairs, handing out leaflets, helping with the teas and clearing away afterwards, while Cynthia did nothing more that swan around, so it was a particularly tedious morning for me. Nevertheless the conference itself was very informative, with the chairman giving out useful advice and contact numbers of the local press and radio as well as copies of a petition for people to collect signatures in their immediate localities, which all helped to make me feel more positive about the future of our little home.

"Shouldn't you be thinking about expanding?" enquired Cynthia during the journey back, while I tried to look elegant in the passenger seat with my chin on my knees. "My 'starter home' was smaller than yours and I haven't been in the business that much longer than you. All the banks are desperate to lend money to people like us. I've already got two 'thirty bedders' and I'm getting a nursing home next."

"I'm not sure I could manage more than ten" I replied tactfully at first, but I couldn't help revealing my irritation and added: "Anyway, small family run homes play an important part in giving the elderly more choice, I've always objected to smaller homes being called 'starter homes' in the business. It implies that they'll keep changing hands and can't provide stability."

"I've never thought of it that way" she reflected, rearranging her hair with one hand and steering with the other one, her arm fully stretched across the wheel.

"By the way Sonia, I'm really sorry I lumbered you with all that work at the meeting, people just kept on asking me questions and I couldn't get away. And listen, don't worry, all over the country professionals are getting proactive, besides, nobody really believes that the new regulations will be imposed on established homes, especially ones with good reputations like yours" and as she pulled up outside The Ivies she continued "In any case, I think you're absolutely right, there's an obsession with expansion, as if it's the only measure of successful good quality care. What's wrong with staying small?"

Then, as she watched me struggling to heave myself out of the famous car, she broke into a sudden spontaneous peel of laughter,

"You think *you're* having trouble. You should see my residents trying to get in and out!"

Any reservations I may have had about her vanished into thin air at this unexpected sense of the ridiculous and I cracked up at the very thought. She couldn't stop for coffee, but we knew we'd be in touch and once again parted on a happy note.

Spurred on by the general mood of optimism, Wanty Wanty and I got stuck into organizing the planned tea party that very afternoon. We hired the main hall at the community centre for the end of August; we got Tess to book her band for the early afternoon event and her singing teacher offered to play some classical pieces on the piano; Joe agreed to do some sing along songs, so we had something to suit all tastes; we advertised the event and started selling tickets within the week and I prepared a short speech.

Soon afterwards we had a recorded interview with the local radio station about how the new regulations would affect our particular home and this went out as part of the news, being repeated every hour on a Monday sometime in early August; we got people to sign the petition outside the library, the chemist, the health centre, the church, the supermarket and the local pub; finally we got an article in the paper and quite frankly we couldn't have publicised our case more widely. Other homes all over the country were doing similar things and eventually everybody everywhere seemed to be talking about the 1984 Act of Parliament. The newspapers were full of it, radio and TV covered it from every conceivable angle and many politicians and public figures were dead set against many aspects of it.

Our tea party was a great success. Danni stayed at home to look after Edith, Bessie and Florence, who didn't want to go, while all the other residents thoroughly enjoyed themselves.

Apart from selling fifty tickets at five pounds each, making a hundred pounds on the raffle and donating two hundred and fifty pounds to Help the Aged, we were able to spread the word brilliantly and get loads more signatures on the petition. Afterwards our local councillor received dozens of letters in our support and came to The Ivies in person to promise to bring pressure to bear on local government.

Then all of a sudden in the run up to Christmas, everything went quiet and the whole subject seemed to disappear. When we rang the registration unit for an update we were told to refer to our last inspection report in which any recommendations made were, as far as they were concerned, within a clear legal framework and it was our duty therefore to comply, if we wished to be registered as required by the present law.

And a Merry Christmas to you too, you miserable old sod.

Chapter 48

The whole month of December was an extremely hectic time for rest homes, as every distant relation, old school friend, do-gooder and his cousin came out of the woodwork, making loads of extra work and causing emotions to run high.

Nearly every resident had inexplicable tearful moments and nearly every resident had unforeseeable ratty moments. Nearly every resident received at least one Christmas card with illegible writing on it, so they didn't know who it was from and nearly every resident had at least one Christmas card from somebody they'd never wanted to hear from again.

There was a constant ringing of either the doorbell or the phone and a constant stream of unexpected visitors. Residents received parcels they couldn't open, presents they couldn't use and hampers full of foodstuffs they couldn't eat.

It was alright for me because I loved Christmas. I loved the sense of anticipation, the decorations, the fairy lights, the carols and everything about getting into the festive spirit. But it was hideous for Wanty Wanty, who thought it was all a load of tosh and a total waste of money. He had a lot in common with Bessie on that score and together they rubbished everything from mince pies to mistletoe in a vain attempt to take the wind out of my sails.

The one unsettling aspect of that particular Christmas though, was the business about the double rooms, which was playing on my mind until Miss Older came up with a marvellous idea and phoned us up one morning while we were having breakfast.

"Could I come over to see you Soneea dear? Nurse Clair said she'd walk me across. I thought ten thirty would suit you best. I'll bring my ciggies."

She could hardly wait to sit down before explaining that she'd found a possible solution to our predicament. Sooner or later, she told us, she was going to have to sell her bungalow to finance her care. She didn't have a family to leave it to anyway, so she wasn't bothered. But why wait? Why not get a valuation and sell it to *us* now? We could convert it into an annexe by building a corridor to join the two buildings. It was big enough for four bedrooms with en-suite facilities, giving us our ideal number of ten residents, which would not only finance the project but give us more security for the future as well. From her own point of view, she'd save money by not paying the agency fee and, more importantly, she'd get to stay in her own home possibly for as long as she lived. She'd got the idea from a comment I'd made when taking her home one evening when it was raining.

"What we need is a covered walkway. We'd have to take a fence panel down first, that's all" I'd said and this had got her thinking. She'd run it by Klondyke Claire, who couldn't find anything wrong with the idea, she'd got Stan's approval and she'd even written to cousin Cyril.

A quick glance at the local paper gave us a rough idea of what the bungalow might be worth and we were confident we could raise the money, so we agreed with the idea in principle.

"If you turn the kitchen into a bedroom and keep the back door in it, I'll have that as my room and I'll be able to sit on the porch and watch Stan do the gardening just like I do now. Ooh Soneea, wouldn't it be nice?"

It was nothing short of brilliant, the perfect solution for all of us, which helped us to stop worrying about the future and, except for the fact that the Captain got plastered at the Christmas party and fell down the stairs sustaining a fat lip and a sore head, we enjoyed a carefree Christmas, our third one in the rest home.

Chapter 49

Early in the New Year, Miss Older contacted her solicitor and arranged a meeting with him and us at the rest home, to discuss her idea. He arrived punctually soon after lunch when there was nobody else in the lounge, the residents having followed their usual routines and Mr Harris having gone to visit his wife.

"Doorbell darlin!" announced Mrs W outside her room, as I made my way to the front door.

"Doorbell darlin!" repeated Wanty Wanty coming down the stairs with the empty coffee cups.

Ignoring them both as usual, I let the solicitor in. He looked much like I'd imagined, rather short and bland, but he turned out not to be the half-wit I'd judged him to be, indeed he was quite 'with it' and extremely polite, treating Miss Older with a lovely old fashioned deference. He complemented her on her sharp mind and shrewd judgement after she told him about her financial position, her current situation and her intention to move into The Ivies when the time came. He told her how unusual it was for people to have such foresight and what a pleasure it was to meet somebody who did. He also told her that he'd done a little bit of investigating and by all accounts she couldn't have found better people to take care of her. That they happened to be right next-door was a stroke of immense great fortune and this last bit was incidentally what exonerated him from his misdemeanour on the phone and put him into my good books. When she told him how the new regulations would effect the home (and indirectly her as well) and how she'd come up with the plan of selling the bungalow to us sooner rather than later to resolve both situations, he pretended to mull it over for a while to be polite before explaining that he categorically could not advise her to take that course of action only warn her against it, because there was a clear 'conflict of interest' and this prevented him or any other solicitor from doing the conveyancing on her behalf.

178

That was the end of our pipe dream and Miss Older was quite bemused. To be honest I didn't really understand it any more than she did, but I did say that any solicitor would only be able to act in his clients' best interests and that was what he was surely doing.

"They're all crooks dear" was all she could say.

Chapter 50

After the solicitor and Miss Older left, Mr Harris returned from visiting his wife and complained of feeling unwell. He had a sore throat and a headache and he thought he should go home to bed instead of staying for supper. I gave him a Beechams Powder and instructions to take a dose every four hours then Wanty Wanty took him back in the car, with Mrs W and the Captain going along for the ride.

I phoned his daughter to let her know and, as soon as I put the receiver down I had a call from Cynthia inviting me to take some residents to the opening of her new nursing home on the Wednesday of the following week. As things turned out though, both Mrs W and the Captain woke up the following morning with sore throats and, together with Mr Harris who stayed at home, developed a nasty dose of flu within days. One by one the others dropped like flies so none of them was able to go and I went on my own. I couldn't stay out for long, leaving Wanty Wanty and Danni as I did to cope with what had turned into more of a make shift hospital in a war zone than a nice rest home. All the residents were coughing and sneezing and in need of a lot more help than usual. One or two developed diarrhoea or temporary incontinence, one or two were prescribed inhalation treatments to combat serious nasal congestion or bronchitis and all needed round the clock attendance.

I arrived at the nursing home early in the afternoon a bit worn out to say the least, wishing I could just sit down at home with a cup of coffee and a magazine, but I was pleasantly surprised to see that Cynthia had found a beautifully converted former convent with a sweeping driveway and an imposing arched front door. Surrounded by lush mature gardens arranged into separate areas with benches, arbours and small terraces in the most luxurious and attractive way, it was quite simply the perfect setting for any home and I was really keen to see the inside.

The 'House Manager' let me in explaining that Cynthia was 'tied up with the chef', which was perhaps not the best way of putting it and she led me to join other guests in a large reception room, where I recognized other members of the association and got chatting to them while canapés and drinks were being handed round.

I didn't get to see the whole home, just a very small part of it in fact, but I saw enough to know that it wasn't the sort of place I'd want to run.

The kitchen was a proper commercial stainless steel affair with fluorescent lighting, electric fly zappers and a constant burring of appliances of one sort or another. There was a sectioned off scullery with no window, housing an enormous dishwasher with wall to wall shelving stacked with trays, crockery and cutlery and, plastered all over the place, instructions about health and safety, fire prevention, first aid and so on.

The laundry room had industrial washing machines and tumble driers the same height as me along one wall; fifty numbered cubicles and other marked shelves for linen on another wall; lists of instructions, contact numbers for breakdowns and reminders to switch off appliances all over the wall with the window in it; brooms, buckets and mops against the last wall behind the door and the floor was littered with plastic baskets and other containers next to a couple of burnt out ironing boards.

The staff room was a pigsty with an overflowing waste paper basket in the corner and newspapers and magazines strewn all over the place. Either side there were rows of lockers, some loos marked 'STAFF ONLY' and 'WASH YOUR HANDS NOW PLEASE' and there was a large fire exit sign further along the corridor, all pet hates of mine, as you know.

Generally, there was a smell of yesterday's gravy about the place and nothing particularly stylish about its appearance except, of course its actual structure. I had to admit, on the other hand, that the residents' rooms I saw on the ground floor were actually really nice. They were larger than your average single with en-suite facilities and lovely big windows overlooking the gardens. They were sympathetically furnished with decent period furniture and they didn't look in the least bit clinical. On my way out, I picked up a brochure and was surprised to find that the weekly fee was much the same as other nursing homes in the area and I concluded that, if one needed to go into a nursing home, it seemed as good a place as any I'd seen.

Walking towards the parking area, I spotted Cynthia's car with the ridiculous number plate, CYN 4U, or whatever it was and I smiled inwardly. Then right next to it there was another car, the same model in a different colour with the number RU4 ME2 and the sight of them lined up together with everything they stood for was so jarring against the serene beauty of the building and its location, it made me think of Cynthia as a joke. I hadn't met her other half yet and I quite frankly didn't want to, but I couldn't wait to go home and tell the others all about it.

Chapter 51

Meanwhile back at the rest home, Tess was sent home early from school with a very sore throat feeling sick, on top of which Mrs W, who was asthmatic and prone to wheezing at the best of times, suffered such a bad attack that Wanty Wanty thought she was at death's door and rang the doctor, something he normally preferred me to do and avoided like the plague.

He and Danni spent the whole time running up and down the stairs in and out of residents' rooms, back and forth to the chemist, reaching near exhaustion point by the time I got back and I did feel guilty especially for not being there for Tess, who was feeling a bit better since taking a dose of Beechams Powders, but by now was gradually losing her voice and heading towards having to cancel her singing commitments for the foreseeable future.

Just like I'd done for everybody else, I poured eucalyptus oil into the china humidifier hanging on her radiator, rubbed Vicks on her back and chest, made up some salt water for her to gargle with and gave her lots of hot drinks. However, it was clear that we not only had another patient, but were one man down for the weekend shift too.

Needless to say, the chaos continued well into the following week and just as one or two people were showing signs of recovery, Wanty Wanty, Danni and I all went down with it as well.

Not surprisingly, I hadn't popped over to see Miss Older for fear of spreading the virus and I kept in touch with her on the phone instead. She was managing well, although she told me that she was upset because Stan hadn't been to do the garden. His wife had taken a turn for the worse and couldn't be left on her on her own. Miss Older was worried about them both, especially as there was nothing she could do to help, which she found frustrating.

Wanty Wanty and I worked through the pain, doing only the absolute essentials, taking it in turn to lie down in between and Tess tried to help whenever she felt up to it until her sore throat developed into tonsillitis. It was lucky we were both over the worst by then, because she was really poorly for at least another week. During this time, which was about three weeks since I'd actually seen Miss Older, I got a call from a hospital social worker.

"I'm ringing about a patient by the name of Ethel Older, who's been put on my case load. I found your brochure in her bag and I see from the address that you're neighbours. Do you know anything about her?"

She'd apparently been taken to hospital by ambulance not long after we'd last spoken the previous week, having somehow fallen awkwardly into her armchair and broken her hip. Knowing about our flu epidemic, she'd called the emergency services without bothering us and directed them to the hidden key in her garden.

"I'm afraid she's not doing very well," continued the social worker, "she didn't need an operation, but she's deteriorated. She may well have had a stroke and isn't responding or communicating. A familiar face might help."

I dropped everything and went over to the bungalow to see if there was anything obvious she could do with. The antique monogrammed suitcase she'd been keeping under the bed ready packed in case of emergencies wasn't there and neither was her bag, so I just grabbed her torch, book and tissues and went to visit her.

Our local hospital was in the process of being rebuilt and as a result the main entrance, from where you could actually see the lifts to go up to the wards, had been locked and relocated to a temporary area miles away round the back of the building where temporary signs had been placed leading along miles of corridors, through the whole width of the place and back to the same lifts. This took an extra twenty minutes of my time, as did finding the temporary parking area and waiting in the queue for a space. When I finally reached the geriatric unit,

184

which had several wards in it, the nurses behind their station were so busy, I had to wait a further ten minutes before anybody was free.

"Could you please tell me which ward Miss Older is in?" I asked a nurse, who looked like a twelve year old and who went off to get a folder and flapped a few pages over without acknowledging me or looking up.

"Oh, you mean 'Effull'" she said eventually in a very annoying high pitch voice and she walked in front of me to show me the way at the same time as she looked at her watch, which was also very annoying. Eventually she stopped at the foot of an untidy looking bed and pointed at the sign above it, which read ETHEL. "There you are, EFFUL," she explained, in case I couldn't read. " Wakey wakey Effull, you've got a visitor."

There was no response from Miss Older and she left me to it.

Poor, poor Miss Older, I was so shocked I could have burst into tears. She was hardly recognizable, catheterised and on a drip, propped up on a pile of pillows, not actually asleep, but her eyes barely open staring blankly downwards, her lovely mop of white hair scraped off her face and so pale she looked practically lifeless. I sat on the bed and held her hand.

"Miss Older" I said. "It's me, Sonia. Are you still with us?" The patient in the next bed shuffled a bit and gave me a disapproving look. I ignored her and continued to talk to her in the same vein.

"What have you done with your hearing aid? You're as deaf as a post without it. And what about your glasses? I could be Father Christmas for all you know, you're as blind as a bat without *them*."

It seemed blatantly obvious to me that, if an elderly patient couldn't access hearing aids or glasses, it would lead him or her to become confused and disorientated, as would being addressed in a different way and Miss Older's case was a typical example of how damaging both these things could be. Nobody called her by her first name, she never introduced herself with her first name and the only people to use her first

185

name had been her parents, her fiancé and cousin Cyril. For total strangers in unfamiliar surroundings to start calling her Ethel (*or* EFFUL), after a traumatic event could, in my opinion cause her to regress to her childhood and suffer from lapses of memory. Add to this her eventual loss of hearing and sight, it was clear her recovery would be seriously jeopardized, hence her present condition.

I was reminded of the day we took over The Ivies when Mrs Morris was slumped in her chair and we had little information about her. I couldn't believe that a similar situation could occur in a proper hospital in modern Britain. That Spit and Gob had no idea how vital communication is to a patient is alarming enough, but medical professionals should surely have known better.

I started hunting through the locker by the side of her bed for her handbag and kept up a bit of banter all the while. Then I noticed that the locker, which was on wheels and doubled up as a bedside table, was a lot taller than it needed to be for a patient in bed to reach anything on the top of it. I also noticed that it was on the left hand side of the bed and I imagined that both things would have been confusing for Miss Older. Not having found the glasses or hearing aid in the bag or the locker, it occurred to me that she more than likely had gone to put them on the bedside table on her right, as she was used to at home, and had simply dropped them on the floor instead. Sure enough when I looked under the bed, there they were against the wall, all in their respective boxes. Evidently the cleaners couldn't do their job properly either. I put the hearing aid in and switched it on, settled her distance glasses in place and by now the patient in the next bed, who was getting a running commentary, was following the events with great interest.

"Thank you. Ooh, thank you" Miss Older was muttering throughout "Mm that's better. I can hear you now. Ah yes, now I'll be able to see you as well."

Then I sat on the bed and held her hand again and all of a sudden she realized it was me.

" Soneea! Ooh Soneea." she shouted in her normal loud voice. "It's you. I knew you'd come. I told them to phone you. I told them you'd come. Oh I am glad to see you. Are you all better? I've been worried sick about you."

The patient next door beamed at me and I was so happy, I could have jumped for joy.

Chapter 52

The social workers' office wasn't far from the ward Miss Older was in. I knew this because I'd been there to introduce myself to the team way back during our first year all decked out in my new uniform, frilly apron and all, for the purpose of handing out visiting cards with invitations to our open day.

I went to several surgeries, day centres, village halls and churches as well and, although I felt really silly walking about looking like a Victorian housemaid, I attracted a lot of attention and achieved brilliant results with at least a hundred people, as well as several social workers turning up on the day and the vacancies inherited from Spit and Gob being filled almost at once.

I hadn't actually met the social worker allocated to Miss Older, but because she'd heard about The Ivies from a colleague, she greeted me with a warm smile and listened to Miss Older's story with genuine interest. I told her about the hearing aid, the glasses and what Miss Older was used to at home and she decided it would be helpful to go to the ward together, so I could show her exactly what her needs were and she could then instruct the nurses accordingly.

We ended up moving the locker to the right side of the bed, turning it to face the bed and taking the drawer out to make an accessible shelf.

"There we are dear," bellowed a delighted Miss Older "torch, tissues, wristwatch, reading glasses, distance glasses, hearing aid box and book, all ready for use." which so made me laugh that Miss Older was obliged to explain the joke to the social worker. She also told her about Wanty Wanty's helpful comment about her bed at home facing west instead of east like Mrs W's.

"Well!" remarked the social worker "You've made a miraculous recovery since I last saw you. Do you remember me coming?"

She didn't remember, in fact she couldn't remember anything about being admitted except ringing for the ambulance, but this was definitely the beginning of her recovery. I visited her two or three times a week delivering get well cards and messages from the residents and Stan, a letter from Cyril, new books to read, clean nighties and anything else she needed. I took dry shampoo in and did her hair, my manicure set to do her nails and I kept her up to date with all the news and gossip.

In due course she came off the drip and the catheter, not before getting a urine infection and a nasty bedsore though, and in total she was bedridden for six weeks until the fracture mended itself and she was able to start physiotherapy. Then I got another call from the social worker to tell me that she was ready to be discharged and to invite me to the hospital to discuss a care plan.

The ward sister's report expressed concern at the length of time it was taking Miss Older to be fully weight bearing:

'This patient is still only able to weight bear to transfer, therefore a period of time in a nursing home with further sessions of physiotherapy will be necessary before she is fully mobile and able to return to her own home.'

Miss Older was convinced that coming back to The Ivies on day care was all she needed and had already told the consultant about the arrangement we had, but the hospital could not discharge her unless she agreed to go to into a nursing home first and I was given a list of vacancies to check out.

I reminded her that it was only going to be a temporary arrangement and we went through the list together. Most were too far away for me to visit regularly, but there were three quite close to the hospital, which I went to have a look at there and then.

The first one was a sharing room with no privacy curtain, which stank to high heavens of urine. Quite frankly the woman who showed me round was lucky I didn't vomit all over her, the smell was that bad.

The second was one of the dreaded long thin rooms with the partition running down the centre of the window. It was on the second floor at the back of the building with thoroughly depressing views of rooftops, chimneys and outbuildings. The third one was so ghastly to look at from the outside, I didn't bother going in. Instead I drove straight to Cynthia's lovely converted convent, without making an appointment, in the hope that she still had some vacancies.

A member of staff showed me into a waiting area right next to a small arched window while she went to announce my arrival. Hanging from the branch of a tree outside was a large birdhouse with trailing ivy all about and on the ground to one side a stone pillar with a birdbath on top. Quite a variety of birds splashed and fluttered about and it was such a delight to watch, I felt my spirits lifting and I crossed my fingers really tight for a vacancy.

Cynthia was pleased to see me, especially as I was looking for a vacancy and she'd just got her new 'Office Suite', which she was desperate to show off. Apart from the 'PRIVATE NO ENTRY' sign on the door, it was particularly nice, consisting of two very large rooms and an en-suite shower room. The office housed an enormous desk facing a bay window with built in seating underneath, a long dark brown leather settee with a huge coffee table and a whole wall covered with beautiful wooden shelving and cabinets housing, amongst other things, a fridge from where Cynthia served us a glass of wine. The second room was a gorgeous double bedroom with its own private terrace for her and her other half to use in the event of having to do a night duty. Both rooms were south facing and it was hard to imagine a nicer working environment.

Eventually I told her about Miss Older, showing her the ward sister's report, and she took me to see what she said was her luxury room and her only vacancy. I couldn't believe my luck. It was a ground floor room with en-suite facilities and its own terrace, surrounded by trellis covered in evergreen climbers. I hadn't seen this when I went to the open day, I hadn't even dreamt of finding anything like it, but I knew at once it was the perfect place for Miss Older, even though it was a lot more expensive than those in the brochure.

And that was how it came to pass that Miss Older was finally discharged from hospital and transported by ambulance to take up temporary residence at Cynthia's registered nursing home, The Cloisters.

Chapter 53

I liased with the hospital and went to The Cloisters at Miss Older's expected time of arrival. I waited in the car for her to be wheeled up to the front door to make sure it was actually her, before getting her suitcase out of the boot and going to meet her. She was really happy to be out of hospital, in particular she was confident about going to a home that belonged to a friend of mine and she was absolutely lucid, although she looked suddenly frail and vulnerable next to the two burly paramedics who were there to accompany her.

The house manager led the way to the luxury room where Miss Older was transferred from the wheelchair into an armchair by the terrace door. She looked out and seemed pleasantly surprised. Within a few minutes Cynthia came to meet her and was especially nice to her and I was confident that things were to her satisfaction. When we were left on our own, I unpacked the suitcase I'd got from the bungalow; I hung six or seven dresses and cardigans in the wardrobe; I folded her vests, nightdresses and bed jackets before putting them neatly in the chest of drawers; I put a selection of books and her knitting on the meal trolley next to her; I took all the toiletries she had in the monogrammed suitcase out and arranged them in the en-suite; then I shoved her washing into a plastic bag to take home with me and finally I put both cases in the bottom of the wardrobe.

"Whatever would I do without you Soneea?" she murmured forlornly in more of a statement than a question "It's a very nice room dear, but it's nothing like The Ivies."
I thought she was being very ungrateful, so I ignored her as I opened the door to the terrace and took in a deep breath.

"Look how lovely it is. Stan will be able to visit on Wednesday and collect your pension in the usual way and you'll be able to sit here with your Guinness, you'll even be able to have a cigarette. It won't be for long. As soon as your walking again, I'll take you home."

"I'm sorry if I sound ungrateful. I don't mean to."
Either she was being uncannily perceptive, as she often was, or
my face was a dead give away, anyhow she pulled herself
together and grinned from ear to ear purely for my benefit.

"Shall we have a cigarette *now* dear? I've got some in my
bag. I haven't had one for ages."
I dragged her in the armchair into the doorway and I perched
on the trellis while we smoked a cigarette together, then I went
to find Cynthia to give her Miss Older's details, order her a
daily paper and pay the bill.

Miss Older's pension had accumulated while she was in
hospital, so there was a fair old sum I had to collect on her
behalf the previous week and in the 'Office Suite', while
Cynthia wrote out a receipt for the two weeks we'd agreed on,
I took both the pension books out of their brown envelope
together with the large wodge of cash, counted out what was
due, handed it over and just as I was about to put the change
and the books back, Cynthia stood up and opened one of the
cabinets behind her revealing the home's safe.

"We'd better keep that in here," she explained, reaching
across the desk "we don't want valuables in the residents
rooms, do we?"
I automatically handed the lot over and she counted what was
left, gave me a receipt for it and locked it all away. Then she
reminded me to take Miss Older's medical card in to her on
my next visit and there was something in her voice that made
me feel like she'd stepped out of her role as a friend. She
opened a folder, started writing and said a perfunctory
goodbye without seeing me out.

I went back to see Miss Older, because she was expecting
me to put her pension books in her bag where they belonged.
She'd asked me to look after the money, being that it was such
a large sum, but she always kept her own pension books. Now
I felt uneasy about telling her what had happened.

"There are so many people coming and going in a large
place like this, they have to be a bit more careful than we do,"
I suggested unconvincingly.

193

"Don't worry dear. You couldn't help it. I'd have done the same."

Before leaving, I went through the list of exercises the physiotherapist had given her to do whenever she could. Some could be done in bed, before going to sleep say, and some could be done sitting in the chair. They were written on a single sheet of paper and described clearly in large print with diagrams. Afterwards she folded it up neatly to use as a bookmark.

She was in good spirits by now and so looking forward to going home, she promised to do the exercises so as get on her feet as soon as possible, eat all the food to build up her strength and keep up her reading and knitting to stay mentally alert.

I in turn promised to visit her within the week, and I told her I'd contact Stan.

I got into the car, put some music on and breathed a sigh of relief.

Chapter 54

As it turned out, I didn't need to contact Stan, because he'd popped round and spoken to Wanty Wanty while I was out.

His wife had died during Miss Older's hospital stay, so he wouldn't have been able to visit her even if he'd known she'd been admitted. He'd organized a quiet funeral, moved house and was just about getting back to normal, her death having apparently been a long time coming.

Wanty Wanty brought him up to date and told him where Miss Older was. Stan said he'd go back to doing the garden on his usual Wednesdays and visit her afterwards.

If my memory serves me right it was on a Monday that Miss Older was discharged and once again Wanty Wanty had been left to run the home on his own, in breach of the regulations. All the residents had recovered from the flu epidemic and were doing really well and it didn't affect them or the smooth running of the home in the very slightest, although it did make Wanty Wanty glad that the Tuesday was his day off.

There'd been little change in the residents while Miss Older was away, except that they weren't getting any younger, of course.

Mrs Morris in room one, continued to think up the most extraordinary names for Wanty Wanty all the while she had the flu. Even she was surprised at them and, in spite of being so bunged up she could hardly speak, the stranger they were, the more she laughed. When she went through a spate of names beginning with 'N', like Neville, Norman and Nicholas, they came out as Devil, Doorman and Dickless, which brought tears to her eyes. *And* Wanty Wanty's!

The Captain in room two, still spent most of his time outside, having chain smoked his way through his blocked nose and sore throat. He'd slowed down a bit since and wasn't able to walk all the way to his daughter's house like he used to, but we couldn't be sure it wasn't more to do with the fall at the Christmas party.

Mrs Swain in room three, was knocked for six by it and, being that she was so frail at the best of times, we needed to spend a lot more time with her than we'd needed for any of the others. She rewarded us by pulling through and telling us more about herself than she would otherwise have done. She told us, for instance, that her husband and both her sons, pilots in the RAF, had all died in the line of duty.

"It was ever so sad," she confided "the boys were killed within a few years of each other and if the *old* boy hadn't followed suit as soon as he did, he would have died slowly of a broken heart, so that was a blessing in disguise."
And she told us that she'd lost them all to their passion for flying long before they died anyway. She said that the last time they'd all been away together, they went to stay in a Trust House Forte hotel called The George, she couldn't remember where. The boys bought her a canvas with a picture of the pub printed on it while they were there, not realizing that it needed to have tapestry sewn into it before hanging it anywhere. She didn't do tapestry at the time and they had a good laugh about it, but she took it up after they all died and managed to finish it before she lost her sight.

"There's a wonderful memory woven into every single stitch, but I never got round to framing it" she explained. "It's rolled up in the holdall in the wardrobe, the only thing I salvaged from the house. I'd like you to have it when I'm gone."
I had it framed eventually and it's still hanging on my wall, too precious to part with.

Mrs W also in room three, got over her wheezing fits and when she wasn't sitting in the window, she was walking about with her hands in the pockets of whatever green pinny she was wearing, eating sweets and fiddling with sweet papers as ever. She still spoke in her own peculiar way as in: "Have one darlin" sticking her hand out to offer you a sweet.

Florence in room four, who referred to the cat treats she kept in her room for Percy as 'chippies', became confused when she had a high temperature and started to get them muddled up with her 'jibbers', hence when she meant to say: "Puss, puss, puss, chippy, chip, chippy" to call him up to her window, she said: "Puss, puss, puss, jibber, jib, jibber." and conversely if you knocked on her door for whatever reason and she wanted to say: "Just a minute, ooh jibber, jibber this leg's punishment," she'd come out with: "Just a minute, ooh chippy, chippy this leg's punishment." which was guaranteed to give you a fit of the giggles.

Out of all the residents, Bessie in room five, who was fast approaching her 104th birthday, strangely fared better than the others and was over her flu without any side effects whatsoever.

Louise in room six, slept through hers and it was the devil's own job to wake her up to get washed, eat, drink and take her medicine, let alone go to the loo and Edith in the same room, nearly lost her voice and her abusive outbursts became less and less frequent from then on. We hoped that this was a sign that she was settled and content.

Finally, dear old Mr Harris, back on day care after a while at home, was so sure he'd been the person to spread the virus in the first place, he felt responsible for every victim and genuinely relieved when they pulled through. I heard Klondyke Claire telling him that it was thanks to the excellent standards at The Ivies that everybody got better so quickly. She knew several in the community who hadn't. It was great to get a compliment, especially coming from her.

Anyway to get back to the Monday, Wanty Wanty was keen to hear about Miss Older and The Cloisters and was really impressed with the sound of the luxury room with its own little terrace, but when I told him about the pension books and the money, which I saved until last, because I was so embarrassed, he was gobsmacked.

"What d'you go and do that for, you daft ha'p'orth?"
I didn't know what I did it for. I didn't do it for any reason. It was a gut reaction.

"It was her pulling a fast one, you mean."

I sincerely hoped he was wrong, but I had a really bad feeling about it.

Chapter 55

There was no way of knowing whether or not Miss Older had any money in her purse. We knew that Stan would be expecting to be asked to get her pension and do a bit of shopping for her and we knew from collecting her arrears at the post office that she hadn't signed the slips for the last Thursday in anticipation of him resuming his usual routine. It wasn't really any of our business, but we were worried that if she didn't actually have any cash on her, she wouldn't get to invite him to sit on the terrace and have a Guinness together.

We suspected that neither the pension books or the money would be handed over without the receipt and we had no way of giving it to Stan, because we didn't know where he lived, neither did we have his phone number. Miss Older specifically asked me to put the receipt in my purse for safekeeping, so it wasn't my fault as such, but I was still feeling guilty for not acting in her best interests when I handed her stuff over in the first place and I was now wishing I'd had the presence of mind to make sure I left her with some money.

"Listen, if she had the savvy to make you keep the receipt, she would have known whether she had any money or not, wouldn't she?" proposed Klondyke Claire encouragingly when I told her all about it, so I tried not to think about it and got on with the job of running the home.

As always, there didn't seem to be much point in visiting on the same day as Stan, so I didn't go on the Wednesday; I couldn't get away on the Thursday because we had our annual meeting with the accountant, which took nearly all day; the Friday was taken up with the chiropodist and Joe's piano session and on the Saturday I had to take Tess to a singing exam, so my first opportunity was on the Sunday shortly after lunch.

The two flash cars stood out like sore thumbs just like before, when I pulled into the parking area of The Cloisters and as I walked towards the building, some other visitors were being let in. They didn't see me coming up behind them and neither did the young nurse who let them in, because the door closed before I reached it, but another visitor, who was coincidentally just leaving, happened to step out and hold the door open for me and I walked in without ringing the bell.

The house manager was talking to a member of staff as I passed the stairs. She smiled and nodded at me, knowing that she'd seen me before, and left me to make my way to the 'luxury room' unescorted.

There was no response from Miss Older when I knocked and assuming she hadn't heard me, I opened the door just a smidgen and peered round. Not only was she not there, none of her possessions were there either and I soon found that the wardrobe, the chest of drawers, the bedside table and the en-suite were all empty, so I walked back to complain to the house manager, who was still talking to the member of staff. She didn't know where Miss Older had been moved to, but after taking me to her office to check the room plan, which was chalked onto a blackboard on the wall and which I noticed had many vacancies marked on it, she found that she was in the 'special care unit' upstairs.

I was instantly suspicious and, never having heard of such a thing in a nursing home where I assumed all the patients needed special care, I asked her when she'd been moved and why. She said she thought she'd been moved on the Tuesday, but she couldn't tell me why, because she only dealt with matters relating to the building, the housekeeping and the logistics of running the home, not the patients themselves. I'd need to speak to Sister Jameson (that's Cynthia to you and me).

I was beginning to feel a bit peeved as I followed her up the stairs and then along a corridor and up a few more steps to a nurses' station in front of an enormous stain glass window on a landing at the very back of the building, where an auxiliary nurse took her place to show me to Miss Older's new room.

My back went up as we passed rooms with the patients' first names written on large scruffy labels, MURIEL, AGNES,

VIOLET and eventually ETHEL. The nurse didn't bother knocking she just opened the door, let me in and walked back towards her station.

The armchair Miss Older was sitting in was facing the window with its high back to the door so she couldn't see anybody going in and just a quick glance around the room made my blood boil. Yep, you've guessed it, long and thin, half a window, half a frigging curtain, no skirting board along the glaringly obvious partition, no other furniture except a bed and a commode and Miss Older slumped in the chair with no hearing aid, no glasses, not even her own clothes, still in her bed socks, her feet too swollen for her shoes or slippers. Her handbag was out of her reach under the sink at the end of her bed, there was no sign of her newspaper, her books, her knitting or her suitcases and beside myself with rage I walked straight out again to demand an explanation from the obviously useless, uncaring, lazy and stupid nurse.

In a patronizing voice without any eye contact of any description she told me that 'Ethel' was happy to change rooms. She couldn't use the en-suite or the terrace in the other room anyway, because both were too narrow with not enough room for the nurses she needed to transfer her from one place to another.

"How the hell do you get two nurses and a wheelchair to help her in that prison cell now then?" I snapped. "And her name is MISS OLDER to you."

I stormed off to Cynthia's 'Office Suite' to give her a piece of my mind and knocked several loud angry knocks on the door. I could have sworn I heard somebody talking, but it went very quiet as I stood waiting for a reply, staring angrily at the sign.

The word PRIVATE was at eye level and the NO ENTRY was underneath and as I stared at the words in the few moments I waited, I suddenly noticed a spy hole in the angle at the bottom of the letter V, then some shuffling about behind the door. I knew full well there'd be no answer.

I walked away from the door, slowly at first, mulling it all over in spite of the throbbing in my chest, and then quickly, my instincts telling me to get to the window overlooking the car park in the reception room where I'd been served the canapés and drinks on the open day. Mine was the only car left and I just caught the tail end of Cynthia's driving off.

It didn't take a genius to work out that she and her husband were up to no good and had left via their back door, through the terrace. I knew I had to get Miss Older out of there as soon as I could.

Chapter 56

It turned out that Miss Older's belongings had been put in an enormous shared cupboard in the hall outside her room and I went to have a look. Whoever had packed them, had literally chucked everything into the bigger of the two cases and probably left the smaller monogrammed one behind. God only knows where that ended up, because we never saw it again.

Resisting the urge to rip the label off the door, I went in to Miss Older and had to repeat the same rigmarole I'd been through in the hospital, getting her hearing aid and so forth and waking her up.

"Have you come to take me home dear?" she whispered.

"I've come to find out what's going on, that's what. This room's a disgrace. What happened to the lovely room you were supposed to have? Didn't Stan see it?"

She pressed her forefinger against her lips and shushed me.

"Walls have ears."

"What d'you mean?"

"That thing on the wall above the bed. They listen in to everything."

She was still whispering, so I started to whisper back.

"What makes you think that?"

"When Stan came, I paid him for the garden and gave him some money to buy some Guinness. We drank it out of the bottles and he took the empties home with him. The minute he left, Sister Jameson came in and told me off. She said alcohol is strictly forbidden and any money or valuables have to be kept in the safe. The only way she could have known was by listening to us talking."

"She might have heard you from the corridor, you've got a big voice usually."

"No I don't think so dear. I can hear it crackling all the time."

"Even without your hearing aid?"

"I had it in for the first few days, just like you told me Soneea, but I'm not wearing it all the time because I've only got one battery left."

I looked at the 'thing' on the wall. It had no switches and no cord. It evidently wasn't a call bell, more a sort of baby alarm and putting my ear up to it I did indeed hear a crackle, so I stood the pillows up against it in an attempt to muffle the sound, much in the same way as Wanty Wanty muffled the fire console when we had the false alarm that time, explaining this to her as I struggled to keep the pillows up.

"I think you'll find it was my idea," she reminded me and we both smiled at the thought.

"I'm sorry Miss Older," I said. "It's not that I didn't believe you, I was just making sure you haven't lost your marbles. Paranoia can be a typical symptom."

"Far from it dear, I've remembered all the exercises by heart and done them every time I think of it and whenever they forget to bring my bag over, I go through all my times tables again and again in my head."

Sitting on the bed next to her as I was, I noticed that she didn't smell very nice, her teeth didn't look very shiny, her fingernails were black, whiskers were sprouting on her chin and her eyebrows were going haywire and all I wanted to do was put my arms round her and cry my bloody eyes out.

"Some friend she's turned out to be," I remarked instead, "moving you without speaking to me first. She's not looking after you very well either, is she?"

"It's like a prison. Two nurses come in every two or three hours day *and* night. They talk to each other not to me. They stick me on the commode and leave me there for ages, even if I don't need to go. There's no bell. They don't bring a nice bowl of hot water like we have at home and they don't top and tail me. They give me a damp flannel, that's all. The food's quite nice though dear. I'm eating everything and I'll be well enough to go home soon, won't I?"

"Of course you will. How's the walking coming along?"

"Not very well."

"Can you stand up yet?"

"I'm not sure dear."

"Have you had any physiotherapy?"

"No, but my hips don't hurt and look, I can lift and bend my legs."

"They need to be put up for a few hours in the afternoon and the bottom of the bed needs to be raised to get rid of these swollen feet." I explained as I kneeled on the floor and took the bed socks off to have a proper look at them.

She obviously hadn't seen a chiropodist and her skin was all dry and flaky, in need of some serious moisturising, but she could do circles in the air with them and wiggle her toes normally, she could also push them firmly against my hands, but when I got her to keep her knees bent and lift her heels off the floor for me to look at, I got the shock of my life. She didn't have *any* heels, only open sores, which must have developed and gone unnoticed way back when she was bedridden in hospital and this was undeniably the reason she couldn't weight bear.

As sad and as angry as I felt, it was actually good news, because it meant that with the right treatment there was absolutely no reason why she shouldn't fully regain her mobility in time.

I asked her to try and sit on the edge of the seat and push herself up from the arms of the chair onto the balls of her feet, not quite on tiptoe and when she did, I held on to her and was able to confirm that she was definitely holding her own weight.

"Brilliant!" I enthused happily "So why haven't you said anything about it? They must be really painful."

She said they didn't hurt, which I couldn't understand because they looked really raw. Instead, she said they were numb. She had no feeling in them until she tried to put one foot in front of the other, then they simply seemed to give way.

I couldn't kneel for much longer and I perched on the commode behind me, looking round for a way to keep her heels off the floor, holding them up by her ankles in the

205

meantime and thinking out loud, when a patient strolled in and sat herself down on the bed. She was in her nightdress, but had a pair of stout walking shoes on and one of those see through plastic headscarves that fold like a concertina in case of rain. She looked decidedly odd. She was about halfway down the bed and just to show you how narrow the room was, her knees butted up against Miss Older's armchair, which she started to brush down with a toothbrush.

A feeling of claustrophobia came over me, as if I were trapped and I stood up, still holding the feet, and shunted the commode nearer to Miss Older with the intention of somehow placing it underneath her calves and freeing myself.

"Arms out," stated the odd looking patient in what I can only describe as a weird lackadaisical way, as she waved the toothbrush in my direction.

"She's right," confirmed Miss Older "the arms of the commode come out if you pull them."

"Oh I see!" I laughed.

Once I'd found a way of keeping her legs up with her heels hanging over the edge, I needed to make her more comfy by getting the pillows the other side of the odd patient, so I edged round her declaring my intentions, just in case she threw a wobbly "Thanks." I said and she simply walked out of the room.

Unaware, or rather forgetting about exposing the listening device, I told Miss Older what had happened before I woke her up. I told her how cross I'd been and how I'd gone to complain and what had happened when I knocked on Cynthia's door. Then I asked her if she knew who took Cynthia's place when she was off the premises.

"There's nobody else dear, only the young girls."

"The trouble is, your heels are badly ulcerated and need to be medicated and dressed by a state registered nurse. If there isn't one on duty, I'm going to have to get you to casualty." I spoke slowly to her in a loud and clear voice.

The odd patient walked back in without the toothbrush. She stood for a minute or two, I smiled and she went out again.

Then she came back and kept coming in and out. I followed her out one time and saw that there was no nurse on the station.

"Is it always like this Miss Older?"

"I'm afraid so Sonia, I think they're short staffed."

"Actually, I think it's illegal not to have a qualified person on the premises in a nursing home. The hospital might just as well have discharged you to your own home."

"It would have been better dear."

All at once, without warning the door opened abruptly and the house manager stood in the doorway, saying that she had a message from Sister Jameson to the effect that the GP had been called out earlier on account of Miss Older's heels. He'd left a script and she'd just nipped out to the duty chemist with it. She hoped I'd still be there when she got back.

Yeah, right!

Chapter 57

I was still there when Cynthia got back because it wasn't three o'clock yet and I didn't necessarily have to be on duty until supper time what with Tess and Liz both working and none of the residents being poorly, in any case I was interested to see what would happen next.

"I'm furious with the staff!" announced Cynthia, barging into the room as if she'd just left. "You'd have thought they'd notice the state of those heels wouldn't you. I don't know what I pay them for."

While she proceeded to medicate the heels from a large box full of various dressings ointments and sterile strips, all of them loose and not in the stapled bag individual prescriptions are usually put in, she didn't say a single word to Miss Older, who was looking at me with suspicion written all over her face.

"Honestly Sonia, these nurses are so badly trained nowadays, you have to watch them all the time, they haven't got a clue, I mean I can't do everything. How are you anyway? You look tired, are you overdoing it again?"

"This isn't about me." I began, without falling into her trap, but before I could go on she interrupted.

"Look, I know you're upset about the change of rooms, I'm sorry, I should have phoned you about it. My more experienced girls work on this floor, you see and Ethel wasn't making any progress downstairs."

"How much progress did you expect in one day?"

"Was it just one day? Tsk, I'm such a perfectionist. If I don't see improvement straight away, I do something about it. We'll get Ethel all better and then she can have her old room back." She was talking as if she was thinking long term and alarm bells well and truly began to ring.

"How come Dr Watson didn't tell Miss Older about the state of her heels?"

"Dr Watson's got nothing to do with it. Ethel is registered with *our* doctor now, in any case she's very confused with extremely poor short term memory, she wouldn't remember anything about it."

Quite apart from the fact that she was really winding me up with the way she kept on accentuating the name Ethel, there was no explicable reason for changing a temporary patient's doctor and I told her so, I also insisted that Miss Older was perfectly compos mentis.

"What's the date today Ethel?" she interrogated without warning.

Needless to say, Miss Older couldn't answer, she hadn't had a paper all week for a start and she was visibly intimidated. As far as I was concerned, she was clearly being bullied and my instincts told me to back off and trick Cynthia into a false sense of security, so I gave her the best version I could of an expression of condescension and changed the subject, saying in the sort of voice you might speak to a four year old in:

"Well, *they* look much better, don't they?" referring of course to the newly bandaged heels "Klondyke Claire would be most impressed, wouldn't she? You'll be up and running in no time at all."

"Yes dear. Will you come and see me again soon?" she knew exactly what I was up to and went along with it beautifully.

"I've got to come back tomorrow. Sister asked me to bring your medical card and I forgot all about it. It'll be in your drawer where you keep your batteries, I expect. I don't know what time it'll be, depends when I can get away."

She knew jolly well that I knew jolly well her medical card was back in her bag and we both knew jolly well that we'd understood each other.

Either the pair of us had been excellent actresses or Cynthia was as thick as pig shit, because she fell for it hook, line and sinker and invited me to her office 'to have a word' over a glass of wine. She then confirmed my worst suspicions without me having to ask any questions. She said that she and her husband were in the process of filling in the forms to get Miss Older the full 'attendance allowance' she was entitled to now that she'd been assessed as a 'nursing case', in need of twenty four hour care. They were also writing to her solicitor with her change of address accordingly and, as named next of kin, they'd be sending him her pension books to take over her affairs.

It was nothing short of criminal. They were seizing the opportunity to take full advantage of a vulnerable old lady and trick everyone into making her a permanent patient. I continued to humour her.

"Have you told her yet?"

"No, I think her solicitor should do that, don't you?"

"Definitely, she trusts him."

"Precisely."

"He'll be impressed with this place."

"I should say!"

Then I asked her if she thought it might be a good idea to raise the bottom of Miss Older's bed and she said the evening shift already had instructions to put bed blocks in place. As if!

I decided not to mention Miss Older's monogrammed suitcase in case I antagonized her and before leaving I thanked her for all she was doing and told her how glad I was to have found the vacancy. What I really wanted to do was chuck the wine in her face and tell her she was a deceitful lying bitch.

Chapter 58

Our recently retired neighbours in the other half of the semi happened to pop over with a bottle of wine that evening and, apart from always being interested in our business venture and all the stories we told them, they were particularly keen to find out how Miss Older was getting on, being that they'd known her, to talk to at least, since they'd moved to the area some twenty years previously.

We told them the whole story about how we'd got involved with her, how she'd come for day care, gone back home again and ended up in hospital and we told them all about the business of her proposal to sell us the bungalow and the question of the conflict of interest. The only conflict they could identify was that, in selling the bungalow to us to finance her care, she'd eventually be giving us the money back because we'd be her 'care provider', which did make a certain kind of sense. We told them all about Cynthia's skulduggery and they said they weren't at all surprised, most home owner's in their experience were only interested in making money.

It was good to have a third party to share it with and it helped to calm me down, especially because recent events, with all the nasty injustices I'd witnessed, had been going round and round in my head and I'd been madly frustrated earlier at not being able to contact anybody in authority, being that it was a Sunday.

In the end it was agreed that I should speak to Miss Older's solicitor first thing in the morning, only then would I know what action to take, if any. In the meantime, we should open another bottle and sleep on it!

It was during this second bottle that they told us about their retirement plan to sell their house, downsize and buy a holiday home abroad and they agreed to give us first option on the property, although they didn't know when exactly that would be.

The prospect of this was a whole new ball game and after they left Wanty Wanty and I talked well into the night.

There'd be no conflict of interest for a start and, apart from the extension, kitchen and utility room, which Spit and Gob had built, the other half of the semi had exactly the same layout of rooms and would give us the potential to turn the home into two units, one for seven residents and the other for eight, without compromising our principles, a plan the registration authority would surely approve of and give us time to put into practice, thus resolving the dilemma the 1984 Act presented us with. It was a definite possibility and we both turned in feeling a little more settled.

Chapter 59

The following morning, on the Monday that is, Miss Older's solicitor was in a meeting so, while doing the ironing in my usual corner, with the portable phone in my apron pocket to avoid the usual likelihood of putting the iron to my ear, I waited for him to get back to me and it was nearly half ten when he finally did.

Yes, he'd received Miss Older's change of address, yes he'd got the documentation relating to her medical condition and no, he was not in a position to divulge the precise nature of it. Yes, he'd have to take over her affairs in the event of her being mentally unfit, yes he'd received the pension books and no, he hadn't been to see Miss Older himself to confirm the assessment. Furthermore if I wanted to dispute her mental or physical condition, I'd need to do so with a physician, which, he reminded me, was not his profession.

I explained that I wasn't questioning the assessment per se, only whether the condition was permanent, which I told him the letter from the ward sister clearly refuted and he responded by asking me what my particular interest in Miss Older was exactly, especially in light of my desire to purchase her bungalow!

He'd turned back into the half-wit and I gave up on him. It was then that Wanty Wanty and I devised a plan to rescue Miss Older.

Going down the correct route, as in contacting Dr Watson, getting the hospital social worker on board, asking for a copy of the ward sister's report (I'd handed mine over to Cynthia), photocopying it, sending it with an explanatory letter to the solicitor, The Cloisters and the nursing home authority, going to the inevitable meetings, keeping Miss Older informed and creating a bad atmosphere for her to live in, was far too ugly and time consuming a prospect, so we decided instead to go down the emergency route and kidnap her.

Chapter 60

Meticulous planning was needed in order not to arouse
suspicion and alert Cynthia to a possible abduction, so we
allowed a period of three days to execute the deed, avoiding
the possibility of failure or the need for confrontation.

On the first day, that very same Monday, I'd go to visit Miss
Older and tell Cynthia I hadn't yet located the medical card.
I'd take one of our folding wheelchairs and ask permission to
take Miss Older into the garden for a cigarette, where I'd tell
her about the plan. I was confident I could transfer her, having
seen that she was able to put her weight on the balls of her
feet.

On the second day I'd do the same thing, hopefully bumping
into Cynthia and being really friendly towards her and
afterwards I'd take Miss Older in the wheelchair down to the
bottom of the drive to admire the location, before taking her
back to her room. I'd bring the wheelchair back to The Ivies
on both occasions and take a few of Miss Older's possessions
into The Cloisters to make it look genuine.

On the third day I'd leave a note in the bungalow for Stan
and ask him not to do the garden but to visit Miss Older at one
thirty, parking his car in the road opposite the driveway, not in
the car park. I'd meet him in her room at two, just as he was
leaving and ask him to wait in his car, then I'd take Miss Older
for her usual cigarette in the garden, walk her down the drive
as if enjoying the views and bundle her and the wheelchair
into his car. I'd walk back towards the car park and follow him
home in the Skoda.

It went without a hitch except for the fact that Miss Older
didn't notice until we got home that her reading glasses
weren't in their case. The final part of the plan was to return
the following day for her belongings so we hoped they'd turn
up then.

Danni and Tess held the fort so that Wanty Wanty and I
could go together. We were let in by one of the obnoxious

nurses who didn't say anything when we told her we'd come for Miss Older's things, she probably didn't know who Miss Older was anyway and she stepped aside to let us pass. We got the suitcase from the outsized wardrobe, cleared the prison cell of all her stuff and not finding the glasses, went to speak to a nurse miraculously on the station. Strangely, she had a lot more eye contact with Wanty Wanty than with me and seemed to take a genuine interest in the lost spectacles and, even though she thought it was very unlikely that another patient might have picked them up, she was easily persuaded by him to check with the 'odd patient'.

I waited in the hall while they searched her room and soon enough the poor old soul walked out of somebody *else's* room carrying a bed sock, weighed down with heavy objects inside. When she went into her own room, I heard Wanty Wanty talking to her just like he would to our own residents.

"Cor, let's have a look. What've you got in there then?" and, evidently pointing at the famous green nail varnish on Miss Older's glasses, "Thanks! These are the ones. Look, green for reeding."

A happy enough ending you may well say, but there was more, because Wanty Wanty put the suitcase in the car and then walked all the way round the back of the building to the south side while I went to knock on Cythia's office door. We'd seen her car and knew she was in the building and just like the other times I'd knocked, there was a bit of shuffling. This time I let myself in uninvited and as I did so, Cynthia was leaving by the back door and came face to face with Wanty Wanty on the terrace. I can't tell you how satisfying that was. We presented her with the receipt for Miss Older's money and she had no option but to open the safe and hand it over. There was nothing on the receipt about a brown leather monogrammed suitcase and she hadn't seen it. If it turned up, she'd let us know. We walked silently out and never saw her or heard from her again.

Meanwhile at The Ivies, Miss Older had written to the half-wit in perfectly intelligible handwriting telling him that she'd been hospitalised, that subsequently she'd stayed at The Cloisters to recuperate, that she was back in her bungalow now and looked forward to the return of her pension books, which she understood had been sent to him for safekeeping. Sorted!

Unbelievable as it may seem, all this actually happened.

Chapter 61

A few small changes had to be made to Miss Older's previous care plan including giving her a new training session to use the commode safely at night and keeping wheelchairs at the top and the bottom of the stairs 'all ready for use' to take her to the loo during the day.

Naturally, she came straight back on day care, but this time we collected and delivered her back in a wheelchair, which frankly was a lot easier and quicker than when we used to walk her.

Dr Watson saw her the day after the kidnapping and he gave Klondyke Claire the job of dressing her heels with a corticosteroid cream twice a week. We didn't need to tell him about the Cloisters, because she told him all about it herself and he mentioned that he'd been notified by the hospital about her injury and so forth, also that her medical notes were still at the surgery, implying that they hadn't been requested by any new doctor. Nevertheless, to put her mind at rest he promised that if anybody other than Wanty Wanty or me informed him of a change of address or GP, he would personally contact the GP and visit the address to make sure she was safe.

She was feeling one hundred per cent better since getting back home, having a proper wash and wearing her own clothes anyway, but this was the reassurance she needed to confirm that she was surrounded by people who cared about her and her freedom and who wouldn't let her down.

She wrote an unusually long letter to cousin Cyril in her usual lovely handwriting. I knew this because she got me to read the last sentence after ending up in stitches writing it.

" All I need now, dear Cyril is for my *heel* to *heal*!"
It wasn't that funny, but seeing her laugh for the first time in ages brought tears to my eyes, helped considerably by the fact that both Florence and Mr Harris had a good old titter once the penny dropped.

She was still on day care in the run up to Bessie's 104th birthday and, with her heels healed, was as independent as she'd been before her long ordeal, except that she needed a walking frame. We were still doing the bungalow run in the wheelchair, more for convenience than anything else, and she planned to go home full time after Bessie's birthday, which I don't need to tell you about because it was identical to her 103rd in every single way apart from the fact that the new outfit her daughter-in-law got, which she didn't wear, was pale yellow as opposed to the previous year's pink.

Two or three weeks after her birthday, when Miss Older was back in the bungalow, I collected the supper trays and found that Bessie hadn't eaten a thing.

"Sorry ducks, I've lost me appetite, I think I'll get me head down."

I turned her covers back and she let me help her to get ready for bed, something she'd never done before and when I put her rollers in her lap, she looked at them wearily, put them on the bedside table and sighed.

"I won't be needing them where I'm going, ta luv," then she got into bed.

She didn't have a headache, tummy ache, sore throat or temperature, but what she'd said made both Wanty Wanty and me feel uneasy, especially as she'd never gone to bed early before and never *ever* without putting her rollers in first, so we decided to check in on her at regular intervals during the evening and we switched off her bedside lamp, which was a little too bright and put the strip light above her vanity unit on instead to give the room a more pleasant glow.

At ten thirty, while Wanty Wanty was doing the lock up, I found her sitting on the edge of the bed wanting to go to the loo. We'd left her walking frame right next to the bed and she was holding on to it as if she might be trying to stand, but her head was hanging down and she agreed that the commode would make things easier. I brought it over from the other side of the room, where it lived as a spare chair, because she'd never actually used it before and I helped her onto it. Then she asked me to leave the room while she spent a penny. When I knocked a few minutes later, she'd got back into bed and looked like she was fast asleep again.

Normally, Bessie had a lot more time for Wanty Wanty than me. She got along with him better and liked his sense of humour, but we both knew instinctively that she wouldn't have liked him in her room for any amount of time during the night, she was from a different era, which we had to respect, so we decided that he should go to bed and I should stay up and check her every half hour.

At about two thirty, she asked for a drink of water and wanted me to stay with her, something else she'd never done before and I sat holding her hand for a good while until she was sleeping soundly, then I tiptoed down to the kitchen for a large cup of strong black coffee and, with the dimmer switch turned right down and Percy purring loudly on my lap, I thought about our first encounters with Bessie in the early days.

She was as stubborn as a mule over any of the proposed changes and hers was the only room we didn't redecorate as a result. She was adamant that she liked everything just the way it was, especially the threadbare carpet and the old fashioned curtains she'd brought with her when she moved in and it was only because her son convinced her to that she agreed on the vanity unit being installed. Later, when the lifting bath arrived, she was reluctant to have anything to do with it and even refused to have her hair washed, preferring to stick to what she was used to which was… to rub it down with her flannel! It was only when I noticed dark orange patches all over her hair and scalp that she let me take a closer look and eventually wash it all out.

It took a bit of investigating, but the cause became clear one day when I unravelled her rollers from the thick brown hairnet she kept them in. They were thin perforated metal rods, the likes of which I'd never seen before, with small bars fixed on one end for clipping into place on the other end, and they were absolutely covered in rust, because she dipped her comb in water to dampen each strand of hair before winding it up. I replaced them with sponge ones at first, then plastic ones, but she couldn't get on with either and became quite cross demanding her old ones back, so I had to buy a tube of rust remover from the bicycle repair shop and scrub them periodically with a toothbrush after that to prevent her hair from coming out in great chunks as it had done before.

"And there was me thinking it was me age!" she laughed.

One day, when I was rubbing E45 Cream on her legs after her bath, which she got to look forward to in the end, she told me that when she was young she used to love all the beauty creams and scents that were fashionable. She said she'd never forget her first perfume because it was in a 'real posh bottle' it was called Jockey Club and she used to take it back to the shop to get it refilled every Christmas.

It's amazing to think that we'd looked after somebody who was born in the previous century in 1881, the same year as Billy the Kid was shot dead, which she was always proud to tell you, and before the internal combustion engine was invented, things that hardly ever crossed our minds during the hectic schedule of running the home.

Anyway, the next time I went up to Bessie's room that night, she seemed a little unsettled and hot, so I opened the window and poured a little lavender water onto a ball of cotton wool and rubbed it gently over her forehead and neck.

"Ta ducks, you're a good sort," she mumbled, labouring over each word and I held her hand until dawn, watching as she simply slipped away.

Chapter 62

The shock didn't hit me until later in the afternoon when I started to feel positively traumatised. I'd never actually seen a dead person before, let alone witnessed death coming and I couldn't get it out of my head. I had to keep going outside to take in a deep breath of fresh air, because being indoors was making me feel faint.

"I hope I go like that!" said Mrs Swain, ever the realist.

I couldn't deny that it was a peaceful, natural sort of death and that I was lucky not to have had to watch somebody suffering. More than that, Bessie had died in her own bed among people she knew well and she couldn't have wished for a longer or healthier life.

There was only her son, daughter-in-law, Wanty Wanty and me at the funeral, which seemed rather sad, but we all dusted ourselves down afterwards and got on with the job of living. They came to take all her belongings away within days and we started redecorating and refurbishing her room not long afterwards.

As soon as the smell of paint was gone, we phoned all the people on our waiting list to let them know about the vacancy. One had gone into sheltered accommodation, one had died, one didn't feel ready to part with her dog and so on. On a first come, first served basis, Miss Older was the next in line, not that we were in any particular hurry to fill the vacancy, in fact not having quite recovered from losing Bessie, it went against the grain somewhat, also the extra income generated from Mr Harris and Miss Older was keeping our heads above water. Nevertheless it didn't seem right to have an empty room for any amount of time and in my heart of hearts I was hoping that Miss Older would jump at the chance, not just because it was a lovely room and it overlooked the whole of her garden, but because I knew it was only a matter of time before she wouldn't be able to cope on her own any more and there was no guarantee of a vacancy when that time came. In the event she turned it down and we did nothing to try and change her mind because it seemed to us that in this instance, there was an unmistakeable conflict of interests.

Mr Harris had seen Bessie's room when it was being decorated and he'd shown a keen interest in it, but we were obliged to honour the waiting list, which he wasn't actually on and offer it to Miss Older, who'd come to us first. He was well pleased when we told him it was his if he wanted it and he had no hesitation giving up his home and moving in. To have somebody who already knew the routine and really wanted to be there from the outset was a treat and he settled in with no trouble at all.

Actually, had it not been for Mr Harris taking up residence when he did, we would have forgotten Miss Older's birthday once again, but when I took his index card out to alter his status, her card was right behind his in the day care section and, seeing her date of birth, I put a reminder in the diary to invite her to tea and get Joe in to play the piano. She was going to be 88 years old, something I knew she was proud of. Before that though, we had the dreaded inspections to contend with.

As tedious as the 'health and hygiene' and the 'fire' inspections were, with all the usual *new* forms to fill, boxes to tick and additional requirements to comply with, they were at least there to improve safety standards, which was reasonable, whereas the county council's inspection for registration was more contentious than ever.

We had a new inspector this time and he took issue with the fact that we'd filled our vacancy with somebody other than one of the residents in the double rooms, which he reckoned was our duty to do, given the advice received at the last inspection.

As far as we were concerned, moving Mrs Swain from her ground floor room where she had a mobile and compos mentis sighted companion wasn't an option, neither would Mrs W benefit in any way from being moved from her beloved window. Louise had already been moved once, to shift her about like a piece of furniture wasn't in the least bit necessary and to take Edith away from her familiar surroundings would have been criminal. In any case, the advice at the last inspection was about what could be done to the *structure* of the place *not* what could be done to the *residents* and moving any one of them hadn't actually crossed our minds.

The new and extremely loathsome inspector wasn't interested in anything we had to say in our defence, not even in the fact that we'd got first option on the other half of the semi, which would resolve any shortcomings in due course, he simply proceeded to measure all the rooms to check the sizes already recorded at the last inspection, concluding that Mrs Morris' room was four and a half square feet short of the one hundred required for registration, being that the old chimney breast hadn't previously been taken into account.

Of all the objectionable gits we had to deal with, this one took the biscuit. He had no place in the 'caring' profession and I doubt he even knew the meaning of the word.

There was some small satisfaction though in the way Wanty Wanty made light of it all, sharing the information with the residents along the way,

"Your room appears to have shrunk, Mrs Morris and you can't stay here any more so clear off."

"Sorry, Mr Harris the inspector here says we shouldn't have offered you this room. Next time you see him coming, you need to hide in the wardrobe, OK?"

Oh and the minute he started banging on about 'indiscretions' and 'non compliance', we didn't offer him any more tea or coffee and Wanty Wanty took the biscuits away.

On a more serious note though, it was utterly disheartening. I mean, surely to God the focus of his attention should have been the residents' quality of life and the type of care they were receiving, never mind the square footage and the ratio of double rooms. In fact, where the bloody hell was *he* when Spit and Gob were in charge, for God's sake and what did his 'all powerful' department do to safeguard the residents from the abuse that was so plainly going on? Nitpicking over stuff that wasn't even remotely our fault was not only ludicrous, it was exasperating and thoroughly depressing too.

To add to our despair, it soon became clear that losing the chimney breast in room one with Mrs Morris in it was not going to be achievable, as not surprisingly, it wasn't just a question of knocking out a few bricks and redecorating.

For one thing it was imperative to install a steel girder, if we didn't want the chimney in room six upstairs to come crashing through, and for another it was necessary to replace the one hour fire ceiling in its entirety, not before arranging for the engineer to disconnect the smoke detector from the alarm system and reconnect it afterwards. Then we'd need to employ the services of a plasterer, have a new fitted carpet laid (unless we didn't mind a ruddy gaping hole in the old one, that is) and finally, marry up the skirting board and cornice to achieve a professional finish.

Had we known that room one didn't comply just that little bit sooner, Mrs Morris could have been temporarily moved upstairs to Bessie's old room and it wouldn't have been so much of a problem, but as things were, there was nothing we could do except put the project on the back burner.

We began to live on a knife-edge knowing that, in the event of anybody dying, we'd not be able to replace them until we were down to six, which meant we wouldn't be able to afford to *run* the home, let alone upgrade the blooming place.

One day, when Mrs Swain was going on about being quite ready to die, as she often did, I told her she wasn't allowed to die yet, we needed to keep her alive.

"I always knew you had an ulterior motive!" she was only teasing, but it started to feel as if it were actually true.

The mutual admiration society meetings began to lose momentum until finally they hit an all time low and both members gave themselves a vote of no confidence and decided to seek professional advice.

Chapter 63

The chairman of the rest homes association was a shrewd businessman who had several large homes he paid people to run, freely admitting that neither he or his wife were natural carers. He'd officially presented us with our membership plaque, when we first joined and had given us his home telephone number in case we ever needed his help in any way. Every time we'd seen him at meetings or functions, he'd always made a point of asking us how the business was going, so he was the first person we thought to ask advice from and he was kind enough to take time out and come and visit us.

"Listen, you've built a marvellous business and you've got the perfect starter home, but that's all it is and the only way forward is to sell it and move on to bigger things."

Then he told us that even with the reduction in registration we'd make a tidy profit, that good starter homes were thin on the ground and that there were plenty of potential buyers. A couple with the husband following his own occupation could make a decent profit from six residents, for instance, and if we didn't put it on the market soon, we'd be in serious danger of going bust.

He was blunt and to the point, but he said that, if we were interested, he'd be very keen to employ us in one of his homes. We could start as holiday relief management and eventually he'd give us our own place to run, with living accommodation thrown in. If nothing else, he suggested, it was something we could keep in mind as a decent possible alternative.

He was very complimentary about us both and about the standard of The Ivies and we were flattered. In desperate need of any small amount of praise from somebody in the know, instead of being totally stressed out by his verdict, as we might have been, we were strangely comforted and very glad that we'd turned to him. Neither of us was interested in his job offer though, as generous as it was, because his homes were all registered for twenty or more. Soon after he left, we got in touch with our financial advisor and he came to talk to us about our predicament a few days later.

We didn't tell him we'd spoken to the chairman of the association, yet he arrived at precisely the same conclusion and he too referred to The Ivies as the ideal starter home. As annoying as the label was and however much I objected to it, in the world of business it was an irrefutable fact.

"The future is in the larger establishments and you'll have no trouble raising the capital with your track record," he assured us.

We said we'd think about it, even though we knew it wasn't going to be the way forward, not for us.

We made no secret of putting the place on the market, in fact everybody connected to us in any way knew all about it and the reason for it. It would have been early in July when we had it valued as registered for six by a local estate agent and Danni did everything she could to try and raise the capital to buy it. She'd always dreamed of owning her own home, but in the end her bank wanted her house as collateral and it wasn't a risk she was prepared to take. At one time Klondyke Claire was proposing to go into business with her and I'm not sure what happened about that in the end. We really liked the idea of somebody already part of the residents' daily lives taking over the business and would have given them priority over anybody else, but it wasn't to be and in mid September we had a firm offer from a very nice couple called Dennis and Brenda. *He* was a lithographic printer and worked at night and *she* was planning to give up her job as a state registered nurse to run the business with her mother.

With the deposit down and the sale agreed, Brenda volunteered to work alongside us as often as she could. She said she was determined to keep things exactly as they were and do things the way the residents were used to in order to make the changeover as smooth as possible, which we appreciated. Everybody liked her, she got on famously with Danni and Wanty Wanty and she was a hard worker. She even came over with me to meet Miss Older, agreeing to offer her day care should the need arise and give her first refusal on future vacancies. Miss Older liked her and was glad that even without us next door, her future was safe.

It didn't take Wanty Wanty and me anywhere near as long as we expected to find our ideal rest home. Registered for ten with only single rooms, all having en-suite facilities, the one sad downside was that it was in a different county and we hadn't planned to go that far. In its favour it had a lovely two bedroom loft conversion as the owners accommodation, with exposed beams and sea views to die for and we didn't muck about with time wasting offers, just the full asking price, which was naturally accepted.

We had a full structural survey, got all the documentation regarding the fire doors, fire ceilings etc, received copies of the annual figures and inspection reports, went to the interview with the registration authority, etc, etc. The only outstanding document required by that particular county council was a full electrical survey report and this was in the post when we gave our solicitor our deposit.

By December it was all systems go, but we couldn't hope to catch up with Brenda and Dennis, who were practically ready to exchange contracts, so we booked a holiday cottage for a month and arranged to put our furniture into storage. We'd have a well-deserved break before finalising the purchase of our 'small family run home' and woe betide anybody calling it a 'starter home'.

Chapter 64

Not much more than a week before the exchange of contracts, Wanty Wanty took Mrs Morris' early morning tea in and found that she'd died in her sleep. She was still all tucked up in bed, just as he'd left her, lying on her back with her arms folded and he was really saddened by the discovery. Dr Watson said she had a massive stroke and wouldn't have known anything about it, but it felt to us like a protest. It was as if she was saying: 'Selling up and leaving? Over my dead body!'

And then, within a day or two, Klondyke Claire informed us that Miss Older had been sent to hospital with a chest infection. I went to visit her while she was still too poorly to talk, so I didn't get to tell her about the vacancy, but Brenda agreed, in the presence of Danni and Mr Harris to visit her weekly to collect her washing etc, as if she were on day care, keeping up the continuity above anything else. It made sense for Miss Older to pay to keep the room just in case. In the event of not needing it, she wasn't obliged to take it, but it was the general consensus of opinion she'd at least need day care on being discharged and all Brenda needed to do was get her to sign her pension books when she visited, to get her fee.

On the very same day that we exchanged contracts, would you bloody believe it, the powers that be reversed the ruling over the ratio of double rooms as well as the size of singles to the effect that it would in future only apply to *new* registrations. All the homes registered before the 1984 Act would be exempt!!!

In effect, this meant that Brenda and Dennis could keep the registration for eight, even though they didn't pay for it, and we would lose our home, our livelihood, every single thing we'd worked our socks off for and thousands of pounds to boot.

Chapter 65

The holiday cottage was in a village by the sea, about a fifteen minute drive from The Ivies. It was a delightful little place on a corner plot with a path leading to the beach and the local pub a short walk away, making it the ideal holiday location. In the absence of anything else, it was the forwarding address and telephone number we gave to everybody.

Before leaving, we gave a party for the purpose of introducing Brenda and Dennis as well as saying farewell to everybody and we finally handed over the business at midday on a sad Monday two or three weeks before Christmas.

I was so bereft, I sobbed in the car all the way to the cottage, while Wanty Wanty drove silently and Tess sat expressionless in the back seat, her arms cradling Percy in the cat basket.

Then, to make matters worse, by the end of the week we still hadn't received the electrical survey report we needed for the registration of our new home and the owners were trying to make us proceed without it, with the excuse that it probably got lost in the post and a second one would arrive any minute. We became suspicious and decided to look for the phone number of somebody with the surname Mulholland, a name we'd picked up from goodness knows where as being that of the person who'd pulled out of the agreement just before we came on the scene. The first of only three listed in the directory turned out to be the one we were looking for and the reason he'd pulled out was the discovery from a reliable source that the home was in need of complete rewiring at an estimated cost of fifteen thousand pounds. Our solicitor tried to negotiate a reduction of the price accordingly, without success, and we were obliged to pull out as well.

Still reeling over the loss of The Ivies and everything we held dear, this came as a double blow and, sitting in the holiday cottage digesting the awful turn of events, the three of us never felt poorer.

To stop feeling sorry for ourselves, Wanty Wanty and I went to visit Miss Older together on the Saturday, dropping Tess off to meet Liz in town on the way.

Miss Older, or ETHEL, as the nameplate over the bed would have it yet again, was recovering well and we were able to tell her about the vacancy, Brenda's promise and all our news too. She told us that Stan had been to see her, but that she hadn't seen Brenda and we assumed this was because she'd been too busy, in point of fact she'd rung us at the cottage every single day for advice of one kind or another and each time we'd spoken she'd sounded really stressed out. Good job she hadn't taken over from Spit and Gob then, eh?

It was quite a luxury to have all the time in the world to visit Miss Older and we took her for a trip round the hospital in a wheelchair, stopping to buy tissues and sweets at the shop and even to have a cup of tea at the café. We left her in good spirits with new hearing aid batteries, reading material, clean specs and news from the ward sister that she'd probably be discharged before Christmas.

Early the next week, we went to the rest homes association annual dinner dance and received the best ever Christmas present in the news that Cynthia and her husband, who thankfully were only noticeable by their absence, had split up and sold up, meaning that we'd probably never set eyes on them again which, as mean as it may sound, cheered us up no end.

"Pity about the number plates!" Joked Wanty Wanty. "The answer to RU4 ME2 was a resounding *no* then!" We got quite merry and went back to the cottage singing 'Oh tidings of comfort and joy.'

Chapter 66

We spent the whole of the following week, while Percy was blissfully curled up in front of the open fire, scouring the pages of The Daltons Weekly for suitable rest homes, phoning up the specialist agents for their brochures, making appointments for viewings and walking along the beach to make the most of our freedom in between. Then Brenda, who'd mercifully left us alone all week, rang on the Saturday to ask what the hell was going on with 'MRS HOLDEN' and how much longer she was bloody well expected to keep the vacancy open for her without receiving any money! Wanty Wanty had gone to buy the papers, so I was the one to take the call and, ignoring her appalling manners, I reminded her of her promise to visit MISS OLDER in hospital and so forth.

"I haven't got time for all that nonsense, I'm not a bloody charity," she complained and before I could say anything, she put the phone down.

I was absolutely fuming, so I phoned Danni, partly to get it off my chest and partly to see what she knew about the subject. I was dismayed to find that she'd actually been sacked for reminding Brenda about her obligation to Miss Older or rather, for asking Mr Harris to back her up when Brenda denied knowing anything about it after moving her mother into room one. There was more disappointment in the news that, when Klondyke Claire delivered Edith's incontinence supplies, which she usually took up to her room in person to be sociable and simply exchange a few pleasantries, Brenda took the supplies off her at the front door and told her there was no need for her to waste time going up and practically shut the door in her face. Nice friendly kind little hardworking Brenda was turning out to be a nasty piece of work.

I went to visit Miss Older the same afternoon, as I'd planned to, and she confirmed that she hadn't seen or heard anything from Brenda. We chatted while I walked her up the corridor and back and I noticed how much frailer she'd become. I went to get an update from the ward sister and wasn't surprised to learn that, as keen as the medical team was for as many patients as possible to vacate beds over Christmas, there was no way she'd be discharged to her own home until there was a guarantee of her going back to The Ivies for day care at least. Given what Brenda had said to me on the phone, Miss Older and the nurse decided it would be preferable to look for somewhere else.

"I should have taken Bessie's room," she confessed " I don't want to be at home alone any more Soneea. Does that sound like I'm giving up?"

"Not at all." I reassured her "I only wish I hadn't lost The Ivies."

"We're both homeless now, aren't we dear?"

"In limbo"

"Mm," she said "I wonder what we did to deserve that...and just before Christmas as well".

Chapter 67

There was a real risk of Miss Older sinking into a bout of depression if another home, even as a temporary solution, wasn't found before Christmas, which was fast approaching on the Wednesday, so I needed to get my skates on.

Reluctant to approach any of the home owners I'd met through the association because of my experience with the dreaded Cynthia, I decided to drive round the vicinity of the hospital, where there seemed to be more care homes than ever, and knock on a few doors.

It was something I could do immediately for one thing and for another, assuming I found a place and she was discharged on the Monday, it would be easy to walk her there in a wheelchair in the event of hospital transport being difficult to arrange at short notice. (I wasn't altogether sure I'd be able to get her in and out of the Skoda on my own.) Miraculously, there was a vacancy in a perfectly nice dual registered home just around the corner, where old people getting to the stage of needing nursing care didn't need to be moved on.

I can't actually remember going to the bungalow to pack for her, but I must have done, because I delivered her suitcase and unpacked her things before going to collect her in a wheelchair on the Monday afternoon, exactly as I'd hoped. I also went out and bought her a golden tray with two glasses and a bottle of sherry to put next to her Christmas tree on the sideboard in her new room, so as to join her in a celebratory drink when she was settled in.

The room was nicely furnished in shades of umber, biscuit and rusty browns, all colours I knew she'd like. There was a large framed picture on the wall, which echoed the same earthy tones as the fabric the cushions were made of and when I first saw it, I thought it was a leafy autumnal design and it wasn't until I was sorting out her belongings that I realized they were cats. Upright cats, upside down cats, horizontal cats, big cats, small cats, fat cats and skinny cats all woven into upholstery fabric, a large square of which had been put behind glass to make the picture on the wall. I just knew she'd find this comical, given her feelings on the subject of cats, and when I pushed her towards the armchair, it was the first thing she noticed.

"Did you put them there specially for me dear?"

"Absolutely, I had them made purposely"

She was really tickled and while we drank our sherry, I brought her up to date with what happened the day before, on the Sunday.

Wanty Wanty and I went to view two miserable looking homes several miles away, both in the middle of nowhere and not remotely meeting our needs and we got back to the cottage feeling downright cheesed off and too tired to cook, so we walked round to the pub for a meal. On the way there, along a route we hadn't taken before and almost exactly opposite the cottage, hidden behind tall hedges, there was a beautiful house on a corner plot called The Willows, which I was sure I recognized as a rest home previously advertised for sale in a trade magazine at a time when selling The Ivies was the last thing on our minds. Wanty Wanty didn't think he'd seen it before and there was nothing to suggest it was a care home of any description, so we mentioned it to the publican to see if he knew anything about it.

He and a couple of locals at the bar confirmed that it had been a rest home in the past, but nobody knew whether it was still trading, nonetheless over a couple of glasses of wine, I convinced myself that it was indeed the home I'd seen, registered for eight with potential to expand to the perfect ten, that the owners hadn't been able to keep up good occupancy levels and make a success of it, that subsequently they hadn't been able to sell it and that the reason everything had gone so badly wrong for us was that this was the home we were meant to have.

"You're moving into the realms of fantasy!" warned Wanty Wanty.

All the same, back in the holiday cottage, he went through all the adverts and brochures again with a fine toothed comb, looking quite disappointed when he didn't find it.

In the morning, in between talking to the hospital social worker and the home owner about Miss Older, I phoned all the agents specializing in care homes to eventually discover that The Willows had just been taken off the market, proving that at least one part of my theory wasn't outlandish. I convinced the person on the phone to send us the property details just the same and, on my way to visit Miss Older, I drove slowly past it to get another look. I was perfectly in love with the place and I knew that Wanty Wanty would walk along and check it out again, just as soon as I left and fall in love with it too. I only hoped it wasn't too late for the details to arrive the following day because I didn't think we could bear the suspense until after Christmas.

"Now that you've got me all sorted out, you can concentrate on yourself, dear. I do hope it'll work out for you. I'll be keeping my fingers crossed," she said smiling.

Just like the time before, I'd collected her pension after getting her to sign her books in the hospital, but this time, she didn't have enough to cover the fee and keep some pocket money in her purse as well, so she had to part pay by cheque. In front of the owner, who was also the matron, she put the books in her bag to go back to the arrangement she had with Stan, explaining while she did so that it made her feel as if she still had some control over her life.

She was very pleased with her new room, she liked the matron as much as I did and I left her, looking as cheerful and as optimistic as I felt, to get back and write to the half wit, send Dr Watson her change of address and phone Stan of course.

Chapter 68

Details of The Willows arrived in the post on December 24th with the last trickle of Christmas cards. Spookily, it turned out to be registered for eight with potential to expand to ten, just as I'd said in the pub that time and I'm not sure which one of us was more surprised. It was really weird that a second part of my wine-induced theory should turn out to be true, although looking back, I suspect the advert I'd seen of the home, whenever it was that I saw it, must have made a deeper impression on me than I realized.

There were no photos of the interior and the house itself was photographed at enough of a distance to render its real life shabbiness unnoticeable. The main selling points were the splendid sea views from all the upstairs windows and the sizeable two bedroom owners' accommodation with private access on the ground floor. The comparatively low asking price was a reflection of how much work needed to be done to both the building and the business itself, which didn't put either of us off in the slightest and, although there was nothing we could do until after Christmas, the dream kept us in high spirits all over the holidays, when we walked past it at every opportunity, even taking Tess to check it out a couple of times at least. Tess had been dreading moving away from the county and was quietly relieved when the other home fell through, The Willows on the other hand was far more appealing to her and, like us she pinned all her hopes on it.

Resisting the urge to simply knock on the door and introduce ourselves, which would have been childish and unprofessional, we arranged a viewing through the agency early in the New Year and, in spite of the fact that we knew not to expect a palace, we were absolutely astonished by what we found.

We both remained speechless as the hoity-toity arrogant owners with obvious delusions of grandeur showed us round the truly dilapidated, sadly neglected, grossly dirty, embarrassingly untidy excuse of a rest home, in fact how they'd hung on to their registration was beyond comprehension, more so even than Spit and Gob, yet we both knew independently from one another that we could transform it into a first-rate establishment and as soon as we walked across the road back to the cottage, laughing at how accurate the rest of my theory had turned out to be, we rang the agency with an offer so close to the asking price, it could hardly be refused.

While we waited for the sale to go through, I continued to visit Miss Older on a regular basis, avoiding the same day of the week as before, or the same time of day to give myself variety more than anything else. She was happy, she looked well cared for and she liked the home, especially the food. The only reservation she had was the fact that, as nice as everybody was, she hardly ever saw the same member of staff twice.

"It makes you feel a bit unsettled dear, to have somebody different every time and they're all so young"
In all fairness to the matron, she made a point of sitting in her room once a week for a proper chat to make sure that everything was to her satisfaction, which was what gave her the sense of continuity and security otherwise missing, but it was my opinion that too many different faces in the day to day caring of an elderly person was not good for their mental health and I tried not to worry about what it might do to Miss Older in the long run.

At last, in early March, we moved into the owners' accommodation and took over the running of The Willows rest home. I told you we were meant to have it!

Chapter 69

On takeover day we were expecting four residents to be living in the home, not that we'd been introduced or anything, or even seen them for that matter, but their names and details were passed on to us by the solicitor of the previous owners. In the event, there were only two, which was probably just as well, because it gave us that much more free time to blitz the place and help with the decorating.

Having sent out our change of address, we soon heard from Danni, who came to lend a very welcome hand and we received good luck cards from everybody we knew.

Long before the place was up and running, we had a call from Mr Harris' daughter Janet. Apparently, after the incident over Miss Older's room and Danni getting the sack, Mr Harris walked out of The Ivies and went back to his house, which still hadn't been cleared or put on the market. Janet didn't find out about it until she went to visit her mother in the EMI Home a few days later and discovered him still there long after he needed to be, just like he used to do before he came to us. She was cross that Brenda hadn't phoned to tell her he'd walked out, as anything could have happened to him and she cleared his room and told her he wouldn't be going back. Recently, Mr Harris' wife had died and he didn't need to stay in the area of the EMI Home any more. Dr Watson recommended she get in touch with us. She came to see us and moved Mr Harris on the same day.

Two or three weeks later Mrs Swain's social worker phoned, having spoken to Klondyke Claire, who gave her our contact details. Mrs Swain's only visitor, her previous home-help, had contacted her because Mrs Swain was as miserable as sin after we left, with Brenda not cutting up her food or giving her the choice to sit outside or in the lounge and not taking her to the toilet regularly, but putting incontinence pads on her instead. The social worker got her back into the geriatric hospital in the hope that we had a vacancy and would go and collect her. I found her in the same corridor she was in when I first met her, lined up with all the others in a wheelchair and my heart sank for her.

"What kept you? You're lucky I wasn't snapped up before you got here!"
She looked frailer than ever.

"Give us a chance," I replied, "we haven't even finished the decorating yet."

" For goodness sake, give me a paint brush, stick me on top of a ladder and I'll do it!" she had the same indomitable spirit and I took her back with me without having to wait for the paper work. On being told that Mr Harris was in the lounge when she arrived she leaned into him and remarked:

"You really can't stay away from me can you?"

"Evidently not" he grinned and they were both in their element.

Then the Captain's daughter tracked us down a month after installing her father back in the annexe of her house, following an altercation with Brenda's mother (who turned out to be an alcoholic) over many a missing can of Special Brew.

"Lack of discipline, old boy!" explained the Captain to Wanty Wanty when he moved in. "Must have discipline, you see."

In due course Florence's 'folk', who were a niece and nephew and had always seemed bland and ineffectual, surprised us by turning up with her in the car and asked if we could take her in. Seemingly, Florence had become distressed over Dennis and Brenda's two children knocking on her door, running about the house playing in the corridors and riding up and down on the chair lift. When she started barricading herself in, Brenda started shouting at her.

Wanty Wanty and I felt so responsible about it all, we were glad they'd come to find us so we could try and make it up to them.

"Ooh jibber jibber, this knee doesn't get any better..." complained Florence struggling over the doorstep, when she arrived "...thank the Lord I got away... ooh jibber... thank the

Lord... I'm not one to grumble... my folk'll tell you, but I couldn't stay there a minute longer... not a minute longer.... who'd have guessed it, eh? Terrible people...terrible people... I knew my folk'd find you... They get me everything I need.... oh lordy, must sit down...."

Veronica came to visit us to deliver a house-warming present and when she saw all the familiar faces, she apologized for not moving Mrs W, as if there was some sort of obligation for her to do so, which we assured her was absolutely not the case. Mrs W loved her life where she was with her window on the world, anybody could see that and, in any case, it was a relief that at least one person hadn't been affected by the change of ownership.

Mr Jones the chiropodist, whom we contacted in the hope that we were still in his area, was the person to allay our fears over Edith and Louise with the news that, when he last visited, he found Louise sitting on Edith's bed chatting to her. He also told us that Edith was unusually talkative while he was doing her feet. In particular he was surprised at her saying:

"She used to be a florist you know. Got her flowers fresh from Covent Garden. Do you know it?"

It made us split our sides laughing and we only wished we could have been there when she said it.

We had no intention of trying to fill The Willows until we'd installed the passenger lift required by the authorities, had all the en-suite facilities fitted, decorated both the inside and the outside and re-carpeted the whole place, but we already had as many as six residents by the beginning of May and life was so hectic that keeping up my visits to Miss Older was getting harder and harder. When she'd first moved in to the dual registered home, the matron had said she was having difficulty managing her at night, because she kept calling for me over and over again, disturbing the other residents and driving the night staff bonkers. I'd been hoping she'd give up on her and ask me to move her long before she finally did. This happened less than a week before her 89th birthday, though she didn't actually tell Miss Older and preferred me to do it. When I visited her, I asked her what she'd like most in the whole wide world and she knew exactly where I was coming from.

"Ooh Soneea, am I really coming home with you?"
She was so excited, she became all red in the face and couldn't stop talking all the way back in the car. When Wanty Wanty helped her out, she was that pleased to see him, she practically stood up without his help and when he put her walking frame in front of her, she held on to it with one hand and on to him with the other. As I walked round the front of the car, she looked at me with tears spilling into her glasses.

"Ooh it *is* nice to be home Soneea. I've thought of nothing else"

"Come on you daft old codger" Wanty Wanty was joshing "I haven't got all day."
Then she was laughing and crying at the same time and I went into the lobby to get a wheelchair, knowing that it was going to take her years just to get to the front door. The Captain, who'd been pacing up and down in front of the house until we pulled up, now stood by the entrance, swaying, hands behind his back, as if part of a reception committee.

"Yes, yes. That's right, this way" he directed helpfully.

"Well I never!" she bellowed in her familiar loud voice "It's the Captain. How nice"

"Must have a cigarette together later," he suggested, ushering her in.
I pushed her into the lounge, where Tess was serving afternoon tea, and passing Mrs Smithers and Mr Brody, the two inherited residents, I transferred her into the armchair opposite Mr Harris, whom she spotted instantly.

"Have you been promoted from day care?" she yelled across the room.

"I'm a fully fledged boarder now" he boasted in confirmation.
Then she caught sight of Mrs Swain.

"Well, fancy that, my old room-mate!"

"Nice to hear you. I never forget a voice," Mrs Swain greeted chirpily.

241

Finally, she realized that Florence was sitting right next to her with the cat on her lap.

"Good heavens, there's Percy! Well blow me down, I never thought I'd be pleased to see you!"

I couldn't have made it up if I tried!

Epilogue

Dennis and Brenda failed to make a go of the business *or* their marriage. They sold The Ivies within eighteen months to a couple who bought the other half of the semi and built extensions into both garages turning it into a 'twenty-five bedder'.

Brenda ran off with one of the builders involved in the bomb hoax.

Tess left school and went full time with us, going to college in the evenings and working her way up to assistant matron, as well as pursuing her singing career getting married and having children.

Danni came back to do her previous shift until her children were a bit older, then she too worked full time.

Liz carried on doing the Sunday shift with Tess until she left school and moved away.

Dr Watson came to see the new home and recommended us time and time again, Joe came back to play the piano, Klondyke Claire to visit the residents and Stan to collect Miss Older's pension and drink a Guinness with her.

We used the same fire alarms company, the same carpet fitter, plumber, electrician and even the same builders, (until one of them ran off with Brenda, that is!)

Within a year, we turned The Willows into a successful family run home, registered for the perfect ten, spanning twenty years until, you'll never guess what, the constant imposition of ever more outlandish and costly requirements for registration rendered it *non viable* as a rest home and we were forced into winding it down, restoring the property into a domestic dwelling and taking early retirement.

A buyer was found for Miss Older's bungalow soon after she came back to us and, whenever the halfwit came to get her to sign anything, he kept a very low profile.

Miss Older seemed to take the sale in her stride and said nothing about it…until the actual day it went through that is.

243

She hardly ate a thing at lunch or supper and was a lot quieter than usual and she spent the day with either her knitting or her book in her lap, staring blankly ahead, without doing a stitch or reading one word. At bedtime I helped her to get ready in our time-honoured way and sitting on the edge of her bed she looked up at me forlornly,

"This *is* a lovely room, dear and I *am* glad to be here, but if only I'd taken Bessie's room, I'd be looking down at my lovely garden and wouldn't be feeling so homesick"

"I know. I can't bear to think about it." I told her with genuine regret.

"Thank goodness I've still got you though" she sighed, fighting back the tears as she got under the covers. Then she stretched her arm out to line her usual things up on the bedside table,

"There we are dear, torch, tissues and wristwatch ....all ready for use."

I said goodnight and, as I walked towards the door in the dark, she added,

"It doesn't make any sense, does it Soneea? So much trauma, so much time and money spent, you lost your home, now I've lost mine....and all because of a conflict of interest".

2480890R00145

Printed in Germany
by Amazon Distribution
GmbH, Leipzig